HOW YOU'LL DO EVERYTHING BASED ON YOUR PERSONALITY TYPE

HEIDI PRIEBE

Thought Catalog Books
Brooklyn, NY

This book is dedicated to my online MBTI community.

To those who have laughed with me, learned with me, debated with me and celebrated with me over the course of the past year.

You all mean more to me than you know.

And none of this would be possible without you.

CONTENTS

THE COMPREHENSIVE ENFP SURVIVAL GUIDE

with an intro by C. Joybell C.

Life as an ENFP is no walk in the park. Despite the happy-go-lucky attitude they exude, only those who share the specific preference for extroversion, intuition, feeling and perceiving on the Myers-Briggs Type Indicator can truly understand the unique form of chaos that governs this type's restless mind. Embodying a profoundly strange stack of cognitive functions, ENFPs approach the world with both the enthusiasm of a child and the wisdom of an old soul. In this detailed, type-based survival guide, seasoned MBTI author and shameless ENFP Heidi Priebe explains how to manage the ups, downs and inside-outs of everyday life as one of the most passionate yet self-contradictory types.

INTRODUCTION

The most common question I get about the Myers-Briggs Type Inventory is "What the hell."

"What the hell is that," tends to be the opener.

"What the hell am I," is usually the follow-up.

"What the hell should I believe you for," is a question the skeptics like to ask and, "How the hell does this apply to my life," is what the pragmatists want to know.

This book is here to answer few to none of those questions for you.

The Myers-Briggs Type Inventory is a complicated system that takes time, patience and diligence to properly understand.

It takes days – if not months or years or decades – to achieve a comprehensive grasp on the cognitive functions.

It takes discretion to realize which parts of your own personality are attributed to your four-letter type and which are just strange quirks that you picked up from your parents.

It takes an infinite amount of effort to understand and infiltrate the world of personality psychology... but it takes almost no time at all to have a brief, unscientific chuckle at it.

And that is what this book is here to do.

This book is here to expose the unspoken nuances of each personality. It's here to highlight your strong suits and poke fun at your struggles. It's here to put you in a box and then empower you to take yourself out of it. It's here to help you share a laugh both at yourself and at everyone else who is like you.

As you flip through this book, I hope you find a little bit of yourself in each of its pages. I hope you recognize some of your strengths and realize some of your challenges. But above all else, I hope you realize that you're not alone.

Because no matter who you are or where you're reading this book from, there are a community of people out there who are thinking, feeling and experiencing life in a similar way to you.

And for better or for worse, we are all in this life thing together.

CHAPTER 1.

DETERMINING TYPE: THE FOUR-LETTER DICHOTOMIES

This chapter is for those of you who have picked this book up off your boyfriend or girlfriend's coffee table while he or she is in the shower.

"Okay," You're probably thinking to yourself by now. "I'll entertain the idea of these personality types that my significant other keeps blabbing on about. But only if I can figure out which one I am."

I have good news and bad news for you.

The bad news is that figuring out your type – with precision and accuracy – takes more time than it takes the average human being to wash their hair. The good news is that achieving a general idea of what your type might be takes approximately five minutes. So unless your significant other has particularly poor personal hygiene, we should be able to get you set up with a starting point by the end of this chapter.

The MBTI® "Letter Dichotomies" refer to the pairs of psychological preferences – represented by letters such as "I" or "E" – that many type-based personality quizzes pit against one another in order to determine one's four-letter type. Though these letter-based stereotypes should not be used as a method of determinately settling on one's type, a brief run-down on what each letter stands for is as follows:

E is for Extrovert **Extroverts:**		**I is for Introvert** **Introverts:**
• Gain energy or 'recharge' through social interaction.		• Gain energy or 'recharge' through alone time.
• Enjoy having a wide circle of friends and acquaintances.	**Vs.**	• Prefer to maintain a small circle of close friends.
• Generally feel comfortable in the company of others.		• Generally feel most comfortable while alone.
• Are perceived as 'outgoing' or sociable by others.		• Are perceived as quiet or reserved by others.

N is for iNtuitive Intuitives:	Vs.	S is for Sensing Sensors:
• Are 'big picture' thinkers. • Are quick to recognize patterns and make connections between abstract ideas. • Are more concerned with theories than with concrete facts and observations. • Focus the majority of their attention on conceptualizing future possibilities.		• Are realistic and down-to-earth in their observations. • Prefer dealing with the physical world of objects to the intangible world of ideas. • Prefer learning facts first and theory second. • Focus the majority of their attention on either the past or the present moment.

F is for Feeling **Feelers**:	**Vs.**	**T is for Thinking** **Thinkers**:
• See a good decision as one that makes themselves and/or those they love happy. • Value interpersonal harmony extremely highly. • Are usually scanning their environments to determine how others are feeling. • Base decisions on subjective truths about how the outcome would make themselves and others feel.		• See a good decision as one that maximizes resources. • Value accuracy over harmony. • Are usually scanning their environments to pick out logical inconsistencies. • Base decisions on objective truths about which outcome would yield the most efficient results.

P is for Perceiving Perceivers:	Vs.	J is for Judging Judgers:
• Enjoy exploring or speculating over their options more than having a decision made.		• Prefer having decisions made to exploring or speculating over their options.
• Work in bursts of energy (often as a deadline approaches).		• Enjoy working toward goals steadily and consistently.
• Enjoy variation within their routine.		• Prefer their routines to remain consistent over time.
• Feel comfortable using unconventional methods of getting things done.		• Feel most comfortable sticking to conventional methods of getting things done.

Chances are, you strongly identify with one or two of the above boxes and feel incredibly torn between a few of the others. That's because in reality, we're all introverts and extroverts, intuitives and sensors, feelers and thinkers and judgers and perceivers.

If we still have time before your boyfriend or girlfriend emerges from the shower, I can explain this to you in more detail.

CHAPTER 2.

CONFIRMING YOUR TYPE: THE COGNITIVE FUNCTIONS

The only true way to determine your type is to determine which cognitive functions you use. Any psychologist, practitioner, author, significant other or motivational speaker who downplays the importance of these functions is wasting both your money and your time.

But what *are* these cognitive functions?

Glad you asked.

Cognitive functions are the technical term for "Mutually exclusive modes of processing information and making decisions." Each personality type uses four (out of a possible eight) cognitive functions, in a specific order. We all use one thinking function (Te or Ti), one feeling function (Fe or Fi), one intuitive function (Ne or Ni) and one sensing function

(Se or Si). Identifying which functions you use – and in what order – is the only accurate way to type yourself or anyone else. The functions necessitate the four-letter type, not the other way around.

Although we all use four cognitive functions, we tend to only explicitly notice ourselves using our first and second functions – known as our dominant and auxiliary functions, respectively. This is because our third and fourth functions do not fully develop until approximately middle age – and even then, their expression is warped by the dominant nature of our first two functions.

To determine whether or not the four-letter type you've picked fits you, take a look at which cognitive functions are dominant and auxiliary for your type and reflect on whether or not those functions describe you. If they don't, peruse the other functions and take a look at the types they're associated with. At the end of the day, it is your functions that determine your type, not the other way around!

The Dominant and Auxiliary Functions of Each Type:

ENFP: Extroverted Intuition (Ne) – Introverted Feeling (Fi)

INFP: Introverted Feeling (Fi) – Extroverted Intuition (Ne)

INFJ: Introverted Intuition (Ni) – Extroverted Feeling (Fe)

ENFJ: Extroverted Feeling (Fe) – Introverted Intuition (Ni)

ISTJ: Introverted Sensing (Si) – Extroverted Thinking (Te)

ESTJ: Extroverted Thinking (Te) – Introverted Sensing (Si)

ISTP: Introverted Thinking (Ti) – Extroverted Sensing (Se)

ESTP: Extroverted Sensing (Se) – Introverted Thinking (Ti)

INTJ: Introverted Intuition (Ni) – Extroverted Thinking (Te)

INTP: Introverted Thinking (Ti) – Extroverted Intuition (Ne)

ENTJ: Extroverted Thinking (Te) – Introverted Intuition (Ni)

ENTP: Extroverted Intuition (Ne) – Introverted Thinking (Ti)

ISFJ: Introverted Sensing (Si) – Extroverted Feeling (Fe)

ISFP: Introverted Feeling (Fi) – Extroverted Sensing (Se)

ESFJ: Extroverted Feeling (Fe) – Introverted Sensing (Si)

ESFP: Extroverted Sensing (Se) – Introverted Feeling (Fi)

Description of Each Function:

Extroverted Intuition (Ne):

This is the dominant function for: ENFPs and ENTPs

This is the auxiliary function for: INFPs and INTPs

Extroverted intuition generates new possibilities, synthesizes abstract ideas and picks up on connections in the external environment. Extroverted intuition is capable of entertaining multiple contradictory ideas simultaneously as it sees almost every side to every situation. It is predominantly a future-oriented function that examines all the possibilities of what could happen next, in a wildly creative and unconstrained fashion.

People who lead with extroverted intuition are usually excitable, entrepreneurial and highly creative. They intrinsically enjoy debating ideas and exploring various interests and they view almost everything in life as a challenge. They are constantly thinking about what to do or experience next, but dislike sticking with just one idea or plan long-term. They desire a life that is constantly providing them with new challenges and opportunities.

Introverted Intuition (Ni):

This is the dominant function for: INTJs and INFJs

This is the auxiliary function for: ENTJs and ENFJs

Introverted intuition seeks to identify the core nature or 'essence' of ideas, people and situations, in order to fit them into a big-picture framework of how the world works. It is a forward-thinking function that analyzes all possible situations that may unfold in the future, in order to pinpoint the most optimal course of action. Introverted intuition is the 'realistic dreamer' of the cognitive functions.

People who lead with introverted intuition are usually intense, focused and highly perceptive of inconsistencies that arise in their external environment. They enjoy riddles, puzzles and wordplay. They often experience 'hunches' or 'aha' moments that they may identify as epiphanies. Their intense foresight is a product of their future-oriented introverted intuition subtly pairing with their inferior (or fourth) function, extroverted sensing.

Extroverted Sensing (Se):

This is the dominant function for: ESTPs and ESFPs

This is the auxiliary function for: ISFPs and ISTPs

Extroverted sensing is focused on taking in the world as it exists in the present moment. It is highly in tune with the sights, smells, sounds and general physical stimulus that surrounds it. Extroverted sensing lives and thrives in the moment, more so than any other function.

People who lead with extroverted sensing are often naturally athletic, highly impulsive and enjoy ever-changing stimuli. They place a high value on aesthetics and lust after the 'finer things in life.' Extroverted sensors are direct, go-getter types – they simply see what they want and take action on it. These types tend to exude a natural sense of confidence, as they are usually quite sure of who they are and what they want.

Introverted Sensing (Si):

This is the dominant function for: ISFJ and ISTJ

This is the auxiliary function for: ESFJ and ESTJ

Introverted sensing is a detail-oriented, information storage function. It takes note of facts, events and occurrences exactly as they happen and categorizes them, somewhat like an internal filing system. This a past-oriented function that dwells predominantly on what has been and it often gives way to nostalgia.

People who lead with introverted sensing are organized and structured, as they believe in being prepared for any potential mishap. They hold tradition in high esteem and believe that the tried and true method is always the best way of getting things done. Introverted sensors believe that the future will repeat the past, more so than any other type. They make concrete plans for the future based on patterns they have observed in the past.

Introverted Feeling (Fi):

This is the dominant function for: INFP and ISFP

This is the auxiliary function for: ENFP and ESFP

Introverted feeling is the in-depth analysis of emotional processes and morality. It seeks to break down emotions to their core and understand them as wholly as possible. It also develops a strong internal system of right and wrong, which the Fi user employs to make decisions. Introverted feeling searches for the deeper meaning behind absolutely everything. Introverted feelers are highly aware of and in touch with their own emotions, and when they put themselves in the shoes of others, they can often feel their pain or joy on a personal level.

People who lead with introverted feeling are compassionate, analytical and often highly concerned with moral issues. They are usually highly creative or artistic, and may feel as though nobody else truly understands who they are deep down. Because their feelings are introverted, Fi-dominant types aren't always comfortable expressing how they feel outwardly. They have a rich inner world that they want to guard and yet they often secretly wish that others were capable of tapping into it.

Extroverted Feeling (Fe):

This is the dominant function for: ENFJ and ESFJ

This is the auxiliary function for: INFJ and ISFJ

Extroverted feeling is highly concerned with maintaining social harmony and keeping the peace within a group. It is a decision-making function that strives to do what is best for everyone and it naturally picks up on the emotions of others. Extroverted feelers often need to know how everyone they care about feels before they are able to affirmatively decide how they feel – their own sense of fulfillment is in many ways dependent on the fulfillment of those around them.

People who lead with extroverted feeling are highly reactive to the feelings of others. They seek out social interaction relentlessly, as they feel the happiest and most alive when they are in the company of loved ones. They seek to maintain harmony and keep the peace at all costs – they cannot fully enjoy themselves unless the people around them are healthy, happy and comfortable.

Introverted Thinking (Ti):

This is the dominant function for: INTP and ISTP

This is the auxiliary function for: ENTP and ESTP

Introverted thinking is an information-gathering function that seeks to form a framework for how the world works on a concrete, tangible level. It is adept at understanding systems and naturally notices inconsistencies within them. Introverted thinking seeks a thorough understanding of how things work – it wants to deconstruct things to look at the individual parts and see how things function as a whole.

People who lead with introverted thinking are logical, systematic and objective to a fault. They enjoy finding 'short-cuts' that increase efficiency within a given system. Ti-dominants are often heavily introverted, as they take a great deal of time to understand how things work before they feel comfortable sharing or acting on their knowledge.

Extroverted Thinking (Te):

This is the dominant function for: ESTJ and ENTJ

This is the auxiliary function for: ISTJ and INTJ

Extroverted thinking seeks to impose order

on the external environment as efficiently and logically as possible. It values productivity above all else and is a results-based, action-oriented function. Extroverted thinking naturally implements concrete plans for accomplishing goals and is quick to make decisions.

People who lead with extroverted thinking are frank, decisive and highly productive in every capacity. They are natural leaders in the workplace as they are quick to take charge and impose order. Dominant extroverted thinkers may come across as bossy or opinionated to those who lack the function, but in reality they are simply pointing out what they believe to be the most efficient course of action for everyone involved.

CHAPTER 3.

THE ORDER OF APPEARANCES

Now that we've either determined your type or thoroughly confused you, let's move onto where you can find your type represented inside this book. In the interest of keeping things consistent, each type appears in the same order in each chapter. The order will be as follows:

ENTP – You'll go first because you lack the attention span to go searching for your type within the chapter.

INTP – You'll go second so that you don't get distracted as you flip.

ENTJ – You'll go third because you usually come in first and some humility wouldn't kill you.

INTJ – You'll go fourth because you're usually listed last and that's unfair.

ESFJ – You'll go fifth because you like to lead your pack of sensing-feeling friends.

ISFJ – You'll go sixth because you don't really mind where you go, as long as those around you are happy.

ESFP – You'll go seventh because that's a lucky number and you probably have an audition to go to later.

ISFP – You'll go eighth because you don't mind blending into the middle and then surprising everyone with your uniqueness.

ISTJ – You'll go ninth because you actually have the attention span to root your type out within the chapter.

ESTJ – You'll go tenth, so you have time to tell the other personalities what they're doing wrong before we get to you.

ISTP – You'll go eleventh because you don't care where you appear within the system, as long as the system is consistent.

ESTP – You'll go twelfth because who are we kidding – you're too busy living your life to read this anyway.

INFJ – You'll go thirteenth because you can be weirdly superstitious and that's a lucky number.

ENFJ – You'll go fourteenth because you don't really care where you appear as long as your loved ones are happy with *their* order.

INFP – You'll go fifteenth because you were daydreaming through the first fourteen types anyway.

ENFP – You'll go sixteenth because we obviously save the best for last.

CHAPTER 4.

HERE'S WHERE YOU SHOULD LIVE BASED ON YOUR PERSONALITY TYPE

ENTP – Hong Kong

Hong Kong offers a diverse fusion of the Eastern and Western worlds, with enough food, entertainment, languages, religions, diversity and opportunity to keep the ENTP intellectually stimulated until the end of time. This type loves exploring new avenues of thought and new methods of experiencing life. The sprawling city of Hong Kong is as diverse as the ENTP's mind – constantly presenting a new opportunity to learn, progress and change. It is the ideal fit for the ever-evolving existence of the ENTP.

INTP – Silicon Valley, USA

Not so much a city as a suburb of one, Silicon Valley is an ideal spot for the innovative INTP. This type thrives in intellectually stimulating environments that encourage both logical analysis and creative inspiration. The massive quantity of tech companies and startup businesses in Silicon Valley allows the opportunity for this inquisitive type to thrive. There is no shortage of brainpower in the intellectual district of San Francisco, which means the INTP almost never runs out of new ideas to pick apart.

ENTJ – New York, USA

If there's one thing ENTJs love it's getting things done – in the most efficient and progressive way possible. This innovative type likes to be exactly where the action is, so that they can analyze the action, come up with a more efficient way to harness it and then turn it into a profitable enterprise that they get to take charge of. What better a place for this progressive type than the center of the world, New York City? They want to be on top of all the latest developments and if there's one place where the action never stops, it is in the big apple.

INTJ – Seattle, USA

As the most highly educated and most literate city in the United States, Seattle offers an ideal fit for the cerebral INTJ. This type is open-minded yet guarded, curious yet hesitant and private yet deeply intrigued by all aspects of the human experience. Seattle itself offers similar contrasts: It is progressive yet secluded, wealthy yet humble and urban yet environmentally conscious. INTJs find themselves perfectly at home in this progressive city, as the science and technology fields attract NT types in hordes. This means they have an ideal peer group to share thoughts, ideas and theories with. Plus the gloomy weather tends to drive people indoors, so the INTJ is free to shut themselves away to work on their latest project.

ESFJ – Los Angeles, USA

ESFJs want to be where the people are – particularly where the people are hooking up, shacking up, breaking up and living it up. This type thrives on connection, which makes the celebrity-ridden matrix of Los Angeles an ideal spot for ESFJs to keep up to date with the latest goings-on. Plus the ever-changing nature of the film industry provides ample opportunity for people-centered work, which is what the ESFJ truly shines at.

ISFJ – Zurich, Switzerland

If there's anything an ISFJ likes it's a clean, well-ordered environment where everyone gets along nicely and everything works the way it should. In the pristine city of Zurich, ISFJs will find themselves perfectly at home. Reserved but polite, the citizens of Switzerland don't like to raise much of a fuss unless they have to. They go about their days, get business done as they should and then retire to their well-maintained homes with their close-knit families. Ever-neutral Switzerland is the ideal spot for the peace-seeking ISFJ. No fuss, no muss, no hefty disagreements.

ESFP - Rio de Janeiro, Brazil

ESFPs like it hot – in every sense of the phrase. Rio de Janeiro is alive and thrumming with music, culture, passion and excitement, which is perfect for the vivacious ESFP. This type likes to be where the action is and where the party never stops. Rio de Janeiro provides unlimited opportunity for this people-centered type to mingle, mix and live it up. Plus the mind-blowing backdrop of the city appeals to the aesthetic focus of this sensory-oriented type.

ISFP - Honolulu, Hawaii

ISFPs are the embodiment of the tranquil, harmonious culture of Hawaii. This type puts a heavy emphasis on aesthetics, which makes the lush backdrop of Honolulu an ideal spot for the artistic ISFP to find inspiration. Collectivistic yet reserved, this type enjoys deep connections with loved ones but takes time to warm up to others – which is why the small, remote location of Hawaii suits them perfectly. Small enough to comfort them, wild enough to let them roam free.

ISTJ – Berlin, Germany

ISTJs like clear-cut, upstanding efficiency – and Germany offers the ideal cultural fit. The historical city of Berlin holds a heavy focus on education, development and intellect, which appeals to the no-nonsense nature of the ISTJ. This type doesn't hesitate when it comes to getting things done and they enjoy living in a city that holds the same value. Patriotic to the core but private with their personal lives, this type enjoys the structured, independent values of Germany.

ESTJ – Shanghai, China

Known as the economic, commercial and financial center of China, Shanghai is an ideal fit for the business-savvy ESTJ. This type thrives on efficiency and progression in the workplace, which means they like to move up quickly. Shanghai offers the opportunity for ESTJs to play in the big leagues of international business, while still occasionally letting loose and getting rowdy in one of the many international nightlife districts. This impressive Chinese city places the hard-working ESTJ right in the heart of opportunity.

ISTP – Queenstown, New Zealand

Coining itself the "Adrenaline capital of the world," Queenstown looks like a giant playground to the sensory-oriented ISTP. This type thrives on hands-on activities and is drawn to extreme sports like heli skiing, skydiving, mountain biking and hang gliding. ISTPs can usually be found dangling from cliffs with a Gopro strapped to their head and complete disregard for the rules strapped to their psyche. They're independent by nature and adventurous in spirit – more or less the precise definition of a Kiwi.

ESTP – Capetown, South Africa

Thrumming with action and adventure, Capetown is the perfect escape for the ever-wired ESTP. Daring and bold, this type enjoys collecting new experiences and moving quickly toward novel endeavors. They are incredibly in tune with their external environment, which means the outdoorsy nature of Capetown appeals to them.

Mountains in the backyard? Check. Surfing two blocks over? Done. The fearless ESTP will find plenty to occupy themselves with in the stimulating city of Capetown.

INFJ – Paris, France

Paris offers an unprecedented combination of class, culture, history and style. The city has been a metropolitan melting pot of artists and intellectuals since its first days and is unbearably attractive to the idealistic NFs of the world. Valuing privacy but feeling deeply engaged with the artistic community, INFJs find themselves blending nicely into the cosmopolitan streets of Paris. They are able to explore their interests in depth, engage with the history of the nation and keep to themselves as much or as little as they please. The delightful French culture of Paris sits well with the INFJ – who is as rare a gem as the city itself.

ENFJ – Florence, Italy

With all of the charm but less of the chaos of most Italian cities, Florence's delightful streets practically beg for ENFJ invasion. The quaint streets and comfortable neighborhoods allow for close-knit communities to form, which is a priority for the ENFJ. This type loves nothing more than establishing deep connections with others and fostering those relationships closely. The family-oriented culture of Italy embraces these values whole-heartedly – with a country steeped in history and artistic creativity to boot.

INFP – Amsterdam, The Netherlands

Tolerance and mutual respect are at the core of Amsterdam's values, which sits well with the peace-keeping INFP. This type craves harmony, connection and deep analysis of the human condition: All of which present themselves in the eclectic city that is Amsterdam. Once you get past the scandal of the drug scene, you find a fascinating well of culture that resembles the psyche of the INFP: Hesitant and reserved, yet deeply understanding of various forms of life. INFPs find comfort in the liberal values of Amsterdam, while enjoying the space to fully consider their own beliefs and values.

ENFP – San Francisco, USA

ENFPs barf rainbows. San Francisco barfs rainbows. It's a perfect fit. But in all seriousness, the liberal values of San Francisco have been attracting NF types for decades. Known for its hippy-dippy attitude and intellectual focus alike, the city is a perfect fit for the idealistic, liberally minded ENFP. This type enjoys exploring numerous avenues of self-expression and personal growth, which San Francisco provides ample opportunity for. This buzzing, vibrant city mirrors the attitude of the effervescent ENFP in almost every way possible.

CHAPTER 5.

WHAT EACH PERSONALITY TYPE DOES AT A PARTY

ENTP – Spurs a massive argument then leaves.

INTP – Smokes too much weed and wanders off from the party, accidentally ending up in the next town over.

ENTJ – Networks the shit out of the party and wakes up with fourteen competitive job offers.

INTJ – Takes scheduled hydration breaks in an attempt to reduce the impact of their inevitable morning-after hangover.

ESFJ – Tells everyone else's secrets.

ISFJ – Spends the evening holding back the hair of whichever of their friends starts puking first.

ESFP – Table dances.

ISFP – Secretly hooks up with someone in the basement.

ISTJ – Stays mostly sober and low-key judges everyone else for acting like a drunken idiot.

ESTJ – Makes boisterous, usually offensive jokes to anyone who's willing to listen.

ISTP – Decides it would be fun to Unicycle on the roof and ends up in the hospital.

ESTP – Gets into a bar fight.

INFJ – Reluctantly holds a counseling session in the bathroom with some drunk girl they don't know.

ENFJ – Frantically scans the room for anyone who looks lonely, then introduces him or her to every single person at the party.

INFP – Tells everyone at the party how much

they love them and then drunk dials their ex and cries.

ENFP – Makes BEST FRIENDS FOREVER with everyone they talk to for five minutes.

CHAPTER 6.

WHAT EACH PERSONALITY TYPE IS LIKE AS A FRIEND

ENTP: The chaotic friend who regularly pops into your life, asks you to join them on a crazy new project or adventure and then completely disappears for 6-12 months at a time.

INTP: The friend who NEVER initiates hanging out but is paradoxically almost always down to chill – as long as you're down to talk science or conspiracy theories with them.

ENTJ: The successful and slightly bossy friend who is constantly challenging you to reach your full potential – because they see it in you, even when you don't see it in yourself.

INTJ: Your friend who's in MENSA and sometimes rubs it in your face... but also has a downright fascinating mind so you're okay with it.

ESFJ: The friend who lets you live at their house for two weeks after you break up with your significant other so they can make sure you're eating, sleeping and going to work like a functioning human being.

ISFJ: The undyingly loyal friend who reminds you of your grandmother but in a good way. As in, they regularly bake you cookies and are always down for a relaxing night in.

ESFP: The friend who is down for pretty much anything, pretty much anytime and is more fun than basically everyone else you know combined.

ISFP: The cool, probably hipster friend who goes to a lot of music festivals and likes everything exactly 6 months before it becomes popular.

ISTJ: The super-organized friend who always shows up fifteen minutes early for your hangouts and whom you'd pretty much trust with your life.

ESTJ: That friend who gives you incessant lectures about how you need to get your life together (and exactly how to do so) but you know it's because they care... or at least you're pretty sure they do.

ISTP: The chill friend who goes along with anything and always somehow knows exactly what's wrong with your computer and/or car.

ESTP: The athletic, adventurous friend who always seems to be off doing something dangerous or crazy whenever you want to hang out with them.

INFJ: The friend you have to plan a week ahead to see (in order to give them time to mentally prepare for the hangout) but then always end up spending ten plus hours discussing the nature of life, the Universe and everything with.

ENFJ: The wise mother hen who's there come hell or high water but isn't afraid to give you tough love if ever and whenever you need it.

INFP: The deep, introspective friend who will listen to you talk for fifteen straight hours without interruption. Of course, when they do offer advice it's incredibly on point and you have the eerie feeling that they've somehow channeled your deepest feelings and thoughts.

ENFP: The excitable yet surprisingly insightful friend who subtly gives you a pep talk every time you hang out and leaves you feeling like you could be the next President.

CHAPTER 7.

HERE'S WHY YOU'RE STILL SINGLE BASED ON YOUR PERSONALITY TYPE

ENTP

You're single because: You're not. You're probably already in a couple of relationships that you've just forgotten about.

You'll get into a relationship when: Your INFJ wife tracks you down and demands to know where you've been for the past six years.

INTP

You're single because: You haven't left your apartment in three months.

You'll get into a relationship when: You meet someone just like yourself on World of Warcraft.

ENTJ

You're single because: You have impossibly high standards and you'd probably just marry yourself if it were legal.

You'll get into a relationship when: You decide that it is practical to do so, at which point you will assess potential suitors for mate value and propose to the most logical subject.

INTJ

You're single because: You over-analyze social interactions to the point where it seems easier to just avoid them altogether.

You'll get into a relationship when: A hell-bent ENFP follows you around for a long enough period of time that you eventually just accept that you're dating.

ESFJ

You're single because: You have a savior complex and keep going for wounded people who can't properly love you back.

You'll get into a relationship when: You're finally attracted to someone who has his or her shit together and doesn't need to be bullied into a relationship.

ISFJ

You're single because: You're attracted to carefree personalities, who then take the relationship twelve hundred times less seriously than you do.

You'll get into a relationship when: The ESTP you've been pursuing is finally ready to settle down.

ESFP

You're single because: You've hooked up with everyone you're mildly interested in and now you're bored.

You'll get into a relationship when: You want to, pretty much. Who can resist you?

ISFP

You're single because: You haven't found anyone you love more than you love Reality TV.

You'll get into a relationship when: Someone intrigues you enough to pull you out of your shell and pursue him or her full-force.

ISTJ

You're single because: You aren't a party animal/ bad boy, which you've convinced yourself is all anyone your age wants.

You'll get into a relationship when: You finally reach the phase of life where other people are as ready to settle down as you have been for the past two decades.

ESTJ

You're single because: Those helpful life

pointers you gave your last date were actually pretty insulting.

You'll get into a relationship when: You meet an Anastasia Steele type who just wants to be bossed around.

ISTP

You're single because: You rely solely on apps to get laid (Mainly tinder) and don't see a reason to switch up the game plan.

You'll get into a relationship when: An insistent ESFJ declares himself or herself your significant other and introduces themselves to your entire family before you have a chance to protest.

ESTP

You're single because: You're having way too much fun sleeping around.

You'll get into a relationship when: You start feeling bad about how long your ISFJ hookup has been doing your laundry for you, at which point you'll finally ask them out.

INFJ

You're single because: You have trust issues.

You'll get into a relationship when: Someone you've known for an unimaginable amount of time finally wears you down and convinces you that you can take a chance on them.

ENFJ

You're single because: You smothered the crap out of your last partner, who genuinely did not have anything left to "Open up" about.

You'll get into a relationship when: You go on the Bachelor and win.

INFP

You're single because: You idealize the crap out of potential partners and then get upset when their reality doesn't measure up.

You'll get into a relationship when: You meet

someone who also wants the rest of his or her life to resemble a Nicholas Sparks novel.

ENFP

You're single because: You have the attention span of a goldfish and cannot decide what you want.

You'll get into a relationship when: You find someone just unattainable enough to intrigue you for a significant period of time.

CHAPTER 8.

HERE'S THE MOST ATTRACTIVE THING ABOUT YOUR PERSONALITY TYPE

ENTP – Your wit

It's not just the quick, clever jokes (though it's also those) – everything about the way your mind works is both refreshing and compelling. You establish dominance almost accidentally through your intellectually rebellious nature and it's insanely attractive.

INTP – Your indifference

I hate to admit it but one of the most attractive qualities someone can exhibit in the 21st century is simply not giving a shit about the dating game. You'd genuinely rather be left alone to your thoughts and to the many emotional masochists out there, you're the very definition of a challenge.

ENTJ – Your aggression

You don't mess around when you see something you want. You are assertive, direct and smart about getting what you want and it's a purely irresistible quality. Your dominant nature is hot. And you make sure that whomever you're going for knows it.

INTJ – Your intelligence

It's no secret that you usually have the highest IQ in the room. Everything that comes out of your mouth is an educated, thoroughly analyzed opinion and it's difficult to champion your knowledge on almost any topic. You know your stuff inside out and backwards – and it's hot.

ESFJ – Your togetherness

You somehow manage to always be miles ahead of the rest of us when it comes to general adulting. You've got your ducks in a row and you're looking for a partner who can measure up. People are attracted to you when they're looking for a partner who's got their shit together and pulls it off with style.

ISFJ – Your composure

You are polished, composed and incredibly humble to boot. You don't demand attention but you attract it through your put-together attitude. People are attracted to your stability and grace – whether you realize that you possess it or not.

ESFP – Your confidence

You're sexy and you know it. It's not just that you have rock-hard abs (though you usually do), the ease with which you attract your gender of choice is apparent in everything you do. You are effortlessly personable and the confidence you have in your own people skills is irresistible.

ISFP – Your sensuality

We're not sure if it's your impeccable style, your quiet creativity or your unexpectedly rebellious side but something about you just oozes sexuality. You are mysterious in all the right ways and it makes people want to know you intimately.

ISTJ – Your reliability

You are the definition of the strong, silent type. People are attracted to your no-fuss-no-muss attitude – they want someone they can rely on and you're the definition of dependable. Plus your dry humor doesn't hurt.

ESTJ – Your decisiveness

It's difficult not to respect your frank, assertive nature. You go for your goals with no holds barred and you don't care who or what tries to stand in your way. Your confidence in what you want makes others want to be the thing that you want.

ISTP – Your aloofness

Your offbeat, somewhat distant attitude is endearing at worst and insanely attractive at best. Despite the fact that you're somewhat reserved in conversation, it's obvious that you're a Jack-of-most trades who can take care of yourself with ease. Your aloof independence is hot.

ESTP – Your nonchalance

You are personable, capable and confident – all seemingly without trying. We don't know how you pull it off, ESTP, but your cool as a cucumber attitude is alluring and absorbing. Something about you just dares us to put ourselves on your radar.

INFJ – Your intensity

There is nothing meek or helpless about you. You are a highly intelligent, highly perceptive individual who understands others on a deep level. This gives you the unique ability to connect quickly with new people. It's an intense experience for those on the receiving end of it and it makes everything about you seem hella sexy.

ENFJ – Your attentiveness

You have this very specific ability to look someone in the eye and make them feel as though you're staring straight into their soul. The presence and introspection that you bring to the table is a rare gem and it's unnervingly attractive.

INFP – Your depth

There is infinitely more to you than meets the eye and your slightly mysterious vibe is compelling. People who meet you for the first time want to know more about what's going on inside your mind – and it keeps them coming back for more.

ENFP – Your enthusiasm

You care more about your latest idea than most people care about everything else in their lives combined. And the energy's contagious. People admire the positive vibes you bring to the table and they want to share in whatever it is that you're so pumped on – hell, they want to *be* the next thing you're excited about.

CHAPTER 9.

HERE'S HOW TO ATTRACT EACH PERSONALITY TYPE

ENTP: Challenge their logic and rebut their manipulative tactics.

INTP: Take initiative. Take initiative again. Repeat until INTP notices your existence. Then take initiative again.

ENTJ: Assure them that a relationship with you is a low-risk investment that will yield a sizeable emotional return. Be strong in your character, but not stronger than them.

INTJ: Present them with a completely unprecedented way of thinking about something they were previously decided on. You'll shake their foundation and win their admiration.

ESFJ: Be popular amongst your mutual peers but make it clear that you often forget to eat lunch or get enough sleep. They'll lust obsessively after the chance to be the one who takes care of you.

ISFJ: Act like a superhero, but one who needs to be taken care of. They'll jump at the chance to nurture your reckless spirit.

ESFP: Look good, make it clear that you're available and then just hang around for a while. Their natural 'people curiosity' will eventually drive them to come after you.

ISFP: Be adventurous and playful and take an interest in them – then give them space to sort out their feelings and come to you.

ISTJ: Be bubbly enough to warm their hearts but scattered enough to imply that you need their help.

ESTJ: Have excellent hygiene and constantly tell them they're right.

ISTP: Infiltrate their social circle, see them regularly, match their level of nonchalance and then put sex on the table.

ESTP: Act sweet, wide-eyed and impressed by everything that they do. Their ego will respond well to your fuel.

INFJ: Be one big, walking paradox. Look them deep in the eyes and tell them that you 'Need them' to help figure yourself out.

ENFJ: Act like the stereotypical bad boy/bad girl but show glimpses of deep emotion–they'll clamor to figure you out and bring out the best in you.

INFP: Act like you have a deep, brooding secret that you're too guarded to reveal. The INFP will not sleep, eat or breathe until they've broken down your walls.

ENFP: Flirt with them once and then act completely unattainable. ENFPs love a challenge.

CHAPTER 10.

HERE'S WHO PROBABLY HAS A CRUSH ON YOU BASED ON YOUR PERSONALITY TYPE

ENTP

Who's crushing on you: The softhearted brainiac.

They're sharp, put-together and secretly harboring a bleeding heart. You're dynamic, quick-witted and tirelessly analytical. You may not have noticed them watching you, but they've been analyzing your every move for months now. This highly introspective type has you figured out in ways that you don't even have you figured out – and discovering this will be a shock to your system. Something about the fierce precision this type possesses will endlessly compel you. You'll want to break their walls down to understand exactly how they tick – except their walls don't come down easily. Both of you love a good puzzle, and figuring each other out may just be one of the most passionate endeavors you ever undertake.

INTP

Who's crushing on you: The class clown.

They're witty, outgoing and goofy. You're logical, introspective and aloof. Something about your standoffish nature presents itself as a challenge to this gregarious type –they want to find out what's under your shell. It may not be a match made in heaven, but it's worth giving a shot. You share a love for the unconventional and that might just include each other.

ENTJ

Who's crushing on you: The scatterbrained genius.

They're analytical, entrepreneurial and just a

little out of touch with the world that surrounds them. You're practical, put-together and high achieving. Though you never pictured yourself with someone so scattered, this mismatched prodigy may just be the yin to your yang. They're enticed by your no-nonsense, put-together attitude. And if you gave them the time of day, you'd quickly learn that they have the brains to fuel it all. Together you could be the perfect team – but you're going to have to make the first move. They keep forgetting to.

INTJ

Who's crushing on you: The emotionally intense one.

They're introspective, analytical and artistic. You're intense, intellectual and emotionally guarded. You may see them as overly whimsical but they see you as a challenge. This emotionally intelligent type wants to break down your walls and understand what's beneath your cool, rational exterior. Though the thought of this may send alarm bells screeching through your mind, don't be so quick to write them off. They may prove themselves imperative to helping you unlock parts of yourself you never knew existed –and you may just grow immeasurably from it.

ESFJ

Who's crushing on you: The scattered romantic.

They're whimsical, artistic and idealistic. You're warm, generous and together. Your compassionate yet put-together persona is attractive to their bleeding heart. With your practicality and their romanticism, the two of you could make a dream team. But you might have to make the first move – they're too busy expressing their affection in their artwork to actually let you know they're interested in you.

ISFJ

Who's crushing on you: The superhero.

They're outgoing, confident and capable. You're compassionate, reliable and organized. No matter how much of a show they put on in front of others, something about you has them weak in the knees. This straight-shooting type is comfortable with going for what they want, but they've been secretly longing for someone to come home to. And you're the exact type of person they have in mind.

ESFP

Who's crushing on you: The strong, silent one.

They're resilient, reliable and steadfast. You're gregarious, excitable and free-spirited. You may not have noticed them admiring you from the sidelines but they're charmed by your charismatic nature and they want to get to know you much better. You two might just provide the exact balance one another needs – they're simply waiting for you to finally take notice that they've been there all along.

ISFP

Who's crushing on you: The nurturing friend.

They're kind, collected and community-minded. You're artistic, adventurous and full of heart. You may only think of them as a friend – the one who's always happy to pick you up after a long night out or relish your latest piece of art. But they've been secretly marveling over your artistic nature and thoughtful presence for a while now. They want to get to know you better – they simply aren't sure if you feel the same way. Drop them a hint if you do – you two may just balance each other out in all the right ways.

ISTJ

Who's crushing on you: The party animal.

They're impulsive, outgoing and excitable. You're steady, reliable and strong. Nobody would ever put the two of you together, but they've been secretly admiring you from the spotlight. This scattered type respects your firm resolve and feels surprisingly balanced out by you. Chances are they'll be moving in on you any day now – they just aren't 100% sure if you feel the same way. It's time to give them something to go on if you do.

ESTJ

Who's crushing on you: The sensible, selfless one.

They're sensible, selfless and sweet. You're motivated, driven and dominant. They admire the no-nonsense attitude you bring to the table and suspect that somewhere below your tough exterior, you're hiding a heart. This compassionate yet self-motivated type may be exactly what you need – their dedication balances your drive and they bring out the soft side in you. But don't worry – they won't tell anyone else that you have one.

ISTP

Who's crushing on you: The whimsical one.

They're sensual, spiritual and adventurous. You're laid-back, logical and grounded. Something about your capable nature is endlessly attractive to their fanciful one – and they want to get to know you better. The good news is, you already run in the same crowds. You'll notice them getting a little bit closer each time you hang out –and don't be quick to write them off. If you do eventually get together, they might just provide the exact mix of sensuality and camaraderie that you've been looking for.

ESTP

Who's crushing on you: The sweet one.

They're unassuming, nurturing and selfless. You're outgoing, adventurous and capable. You may not have noticed them admiring you from the sidelines but once you do, you'll have no idea how you ever missed them. You'll be pleasantly surprised by their sweetness and genuineness. This nurturing type sincerely wants what's best for you and in exchange they ask only that you light up their life with your haphazard charm. They'll be your soft place to fall if you'll be their superhero – together, the two of you could make a dream team.

INFJ

Who's crushing on you: The intellectual badass.

They're intense, unconventional and into pushing boundaries. You're composed, introspective and guarded. This type is simultaneously your worst nightmare and your dream come true. They won't be shy in approaching you and trying to get down to the bottom of what makes you tick. They're natural puzzle-solvers and your eloquent composure is one giant question mark to them. They want to break down your walls and show you a whole new world – one that may just be thrilling in all the right ways, if you let it be.

ENFJ

Who's crushing on you: The artistic one.

They're creative, individualistic and a little bit head-in-the-clouds. You're warm, put-together and nurturing. They're taking their time to approach you, to the point where you may not even have noticed that they're crushing. But this highly introspective type is drawn to your organized, empathetic nature. Even if you haven't spoken yet, chances are they have a painting, poem or song that they composed with you in mind. You inspire them and they could do the same for you. Just give them some time to move in closer – their emotional depth will intoxicate and challenge you.

INFP

Who's crushing on you: The together one.

They're organized, capable and kind. You're intense, analytical and a wee bit out of touch with the world that surrounds you. And something about your accidental aloofness is insanely attractive to them. This kind, nurturing type has been admiring you for the depth and authenticity you bring to every task you undertake. They know that with your vision and their practical skills, the two of you could make a dream team. Now if you'd only stop pursuing all those other tortured artists for long enough to notice them...

ENFP

Who's crushing on you: The quiet, nerdy one.

They're focused, composed and together. You're scattered, enthusiastic and charming. At a first glance it might not be a match made in heaven but something about your quick wit and fearless charisma keeps drawing them back to you. Try giving this combination a shot – you may be surprised to find that their intensity and firmness balances you out in all the right ways.

CHAPTER 11.

WHAT EACH PERSONALITY TYPE DOES IF THEY LIKE YOU

ENTP: Finds out exactly what makes you tick and then uses it to convince you that YOU like THEM.

INTP: Is actually motivated to spend time with you, especially if they don't know you very well. Stares at you when you're talking as though they are studying you.

ENTJ: Takes you out to dinner and grills you about your long-term goals.

INTJ: Lets you touch them without cringing. And/or replies "Yes" when asked directly whether or not they like you.

ESFJ: Asks you ten thousand questions about

yourself and remembers every. Single. Answer.

ISFJ: Develops a keen interest in everything you've ever even remotely mentioned liking.

ESFP: Puts X's at the end of all text messages and finds fifteen excuses a day to hug you.

ISFP: Inserts themselves into the same social circle as you and parties with you regularly until the two of you inevitably hook up.

ISTJ: Rearranges their schedule in order to spend more time around you but fiercely denies their attraction until you make it clear as day that *you're* interested in *them*.

ESTJ: Orders you to go on a date with them.

ISTP: Becomes uncharacteristically protective of you.

ESTP: Shows off in front of you at every available opportunity.

INFJ: Gives you a look that implies they are staring directly into your soul without collecting $200 or passing "Go."

ENFJ: Somehow gets you to open up about your deepest childhood trauma over coffee.

INFP: Writes about you on their secret blog while fantasizing that you've been following it all along and will write them back.

ENFP: Teases you mercilessly and uncharacteristically does not flake on any of your plans.

CHAPTER 12.

HERE'S WHAT YOU SHOULD DO FOR A FIRST DATE BASED ON YOUR MYERS-BRIGGS PERSONALITY TYPE

ENTP – Visit An Escape Room.

You're all about solving puzzles and your date shouldn't be the only thing you're picking apart for clues. By visiting a local escape room, you can showcase your ability to think under pressure and solve the seemingly unsolvable. You'll be energized by the challenge and can bond with your date over solving it. After all, there's nothing more attractive to you than a partner who can keep up with your fast-paced mind.

INTP - Go Star Gazing Together.

If there's anything you hate, it's small talk. You're most confident when you're discussing a topic you're highly knowledgeable about and with a little bit of research, the galaxy above us can be exactly that. Take your date out for a laid-back date where you check out the stars and 'wow' them with the science behind the sights. If the season is right, catch a meteor shower while you're at it!

ENTJ - Take A Class Together.

You're all about progressing and learning new skills – and you want a partner who shares those values. Try a cooking class, an improv class or even a language class – you can bond with your date over your developing skill and learn something new while you're at it! Best case scenario you find love – worst case scenario you've picked up one more skill that puts you ahead of the game. You can't lose!

INTJ - Attend A Lecture Or TED Talk Together.

If this sounds boring to your date, they're

probably not the date for you. You're all about learning new perspectives, which is why intellectual environments inspire you. You can fuel your minds and then discuss the topic after the fact. You'll learn more than the usual niceties about one another and even if the date goes badly, you'll have learned something from the evening – which means it wasn't a waste at all.

ESFJ – Visit A Local Farmer's Market And Cook A Meal Together.

You're deeply connected to your community and the ideal date for you starts at home – by checking out what's happening locally and welcoming your date into your world. You can chat in a natural setting as you prepare food together and then try it out – your culinary skills and your people skills will shine through with ease as you create and experiment together.

ISFJ – Go Wine Tasting Together.

Quality is more important than quantity to you – this applies to both drinking and dating.

Going wine tasting together gives you an opportunity to bond over a new experience – and it's classy as hell. You can scope out your date's etiquette and impress them with your pre-existing knowledge. Plus the drinks will help you both loosen up.

ESFP – Go To A Karaoke Bar.

They call you 'The Performer' for a reason – you aren't shy about getting up on stage and showing the audience what you've got! Karaoke gives you the chance to get silly with your date and lets both of you show off a little. If they're too inhibited to try it, chances are they aren't the partner for you – you need someone who knows how to have fun and who can keep up with your free-spirited nature.

ISFP – Go To A Flea Market Or Bazaar.

You're all about discovering the new and unusual – and markets are the perfect place to do just that. You can hunt for undiscovered treasures with your date – you'll learn quickly whether you love or hate their taste and you can share your own unique flare with them. Plus the strange objects you inevitably come across make for great conversation starters.

ISTJ – Visit A Museum Together.

You're an information sponge and once you learn something new you never forget it. Take your date to a local museum and impress them with your intricate knowledge of all that lies inside. They'll be impressed by your diligence and the artifacts will provide plenty of go-to conversation pieces.

ESTJ – Attend Trivia Night At A Local Bar.

You're a natural when it comes to remembering facts – which is why Trivia night is your time to shine. You get to have fun with your date in a way that engages your competitive spirit and allows you to show off a little. The two of you can bond over your desire to win – and celebrate once you inevitably do.

ISTP – Try A New Sport Together.

Take your date kayaking, mountain biking or rock climbing to bring out their athletic side – you love new physical pursuits and you want a partner who feels the same way. There's nothing sexier to you than an adventurous date and what better a way to gage someone's spirit of adventure than by trying a new physical challenge together?

ESTP – Go Geocaching.

You have an adventurous spirit and it's important to you that any potential partner can keep up. Geocaching offers a fun challenge that plays up your outdoorsy nature and gives your natural strengths the chance to shine through. It's a fun challenge that will set you apart from all the people they've been 'grabbing a coffee' with.

INFJ – Visit A Used Bookstore Together.

You're looking for an intellectual partner and as far as you're concerned, there's no better judge of character than what someone likes to read. You can peruse the shelves together and swap literary suggestions – you'll walk away with a new appreciation of your date and a list of new things to read. It's simply win-win.

ENFJ – Volunteer Together.

Your friendly, giving nature defines who you are – and what better a way to connect with a date than by giving back to the community that you care about together? You'll quickly see if your date shares your philanthropic nature and if they do, they'll only become that much more attractive in your eyes.

INFP – Attend A Poetry Open Mic Night.

Your creativity is your most attractive trait – and what better a way to highlight that than at an event specifically geared toward artistic expression? You and your date can discuss your favorite readings, brainstorm new ideas and maybe even present your own work if one (or both) of you is feeling bold. It's a great way to get to know each other beyond the surface level – which is extremely important for INFPs.

ENFP – Go To An Improv Comedy Show.

Having fun with your date is important to you – and nothing's more attractive than someone with a sharp mind. Visiting an improv comedy show will lighten both of you up and get you laughing – you'll be able to see whether your senses of humor line up and who knows – maybe they'll need a volunteer to go up on stage! You can impress your date with your own quick wit or better yet, give them a chance to showcase theirs.

CHAPTER 13.

THE TOP RELATIONSHIP DEALBREAKER FOR EACH MYERS-BRIGGS PERSONALITY TYPE

ENTP: Boredom.

ENTPs are curious, explorative and eager to push boundaries. They approach relationships the way they approach everything else – with curiosity and an unquenchable enthusiasm to learn more. There is nothing more exciting to an ENTP than a person they can't quite figure out – and there's nothing more boring to them than someone they can. This type enjoys complicated, multi-dimensional partners who challenge them intellectually. Someone who is consistent to the point of rigidity gives the

ENTP nothing to explore and learn from – which means the ENTP will likely tire of them quickly.

INTP: A partner who cannot think critically.

INTPs are the ultimate critical thinkers – this type won't accept any thought, fact or opinion until they've examined it thoroughly, from every available angle. Though they may not expect their partners to be as intellectually thorough as they are, they need to be paired with someone who wants to learn, advance and grow alongside them. After all, if the INTP can't discuss the latest theory they're interested in, they're going to have very little left to discuss.

ENTJ: Disloyalty.

ENTJs show their love through acts of diligence and loyalty – and they expect the same back from their partners. To an ENTJ, love is a verb, not a feeling. The moment they suspect that a partner may be willing to betray or act against them, they will not hesitate to shut them out. Relationships are a matter of risk management to the ENTJ and if you're not going to play devotedly for their team, you can find another.

INTJ: Dishonesty.

INTJs seek the truth at all costs – and their relationships are no exception to this rule. INTJs loathe being duped, lied to or kept in the dark. They want to make all decisions about their relationships from an informed perspective – and if they feel as though they're lacking that perspective, they'll be quick to leave any partner who won't be upfront and honest with them.

ESFJ: Unwillingness to commit.

ESFJs take their love lives seriously. This organized type always has one eye on the future and they need a partner who can keep up. They plan for the long-term – so if you can't see yourself in their future, you can see yourself out of their lives. ESFJs don't have the patience for flakiness or uncertainty – if they're in a relationship they're all in and they expect the same from their partners.

ISFJ: Insensitivity.

ISFJs need a partner they can relax with and feel comfortable around – and being a sensitive type by nature, that means they need a partner who cares deeply about both their feelings and the feelings of others. Obnoxious or arrogant personalities don't fly with this kind and collected type – they put their best foot forward for others and they need a partner who can and will do the same.

ESFP: Having limits placed on their socializing.

ESFPs are the ultimate people-people. It's incredibly important for this type to be able to maintain a wide, active social circle outside of their relationship – and a partner who wants to place limits on that circle isn't going to last long with the ESFP. This free-spirited type needs to feel connected to a community. A jealous or controlling partner who can't handle them socializing outside of the relationship is a definite deal breaker for this type.

ISFP: Being unable to express their true selves.

ISFPs are wildly creative and difficult to get to know well. More than anything else, this type wants a partner who takes the time to get to know them on a deep level and accept them exactly as they are. If the ISFP feels uncomfortable or unable to express who they truly are within a relationship, they will see little use in continuing it.

ISTJ: Deviance from their personal system of values.

ISTJs are incredibly principled individuals who base all of their decisions on a core set of values. And they need a partner who lives his or her life in accordance with those same values, or else they'll have trouble finding common ground. This type needs to feel a mutual respect for whoever they're in a relationship with and if they perceive the other person to be morally corrupt in some way, the ISTJ will have a difficult time mustering that respect.

ESTJ: Inconsistency.

ESTJs take a pragmatic approach to everything and relationships are no exception. This type wants a partner they can rely on to be loyal, devoted and committed. If they perceive excessive inconsistencies within a person's actions over a period of time, they are likely to feel distrustful towards them – and consider them unsuitable for long-term partnership.

ISTP: Insecurity.

ISTPs make for incredibly independent partners and they need to be paired with someone who understands this. They love and care for their partners, but they aren't interested in constantly reassuring them of such – if their loved ones can't take their actions as expressions of love, the ISTP won't have the patience to carry on the relationship.

ESTP: Dormancy.

ESTPs are action-oriented folk and they need someone who can keep up. It's not that they need you to be a marathon runner or a trade skydiver to date them, but do they need someone who's open and adaptable to their fast-paced lifestyle. ESTPs can't handle a partner who only wants to sit at home and deliberate – this type wants to be where the action is and they need someone who is willing and eager to join them.

INFJ: Feeling unable to fully trust their partner.

INFJs are long-term oriented individuals who invest their emotions carefully. They aren't looking for a partner who might bail or run out on them at a moment's notice – they need someone they can trust to stick around for the long haul. When entering a new relationship, INFJs are consistently evaluating whether or not their partner is someone they can safely invest their love in long-term – and if they get the sense that they aren't, they won't waste any more time on the relationship.

ENFJ: Feeling unneeded.

ENFJs live to give to others. This generous type serves a well of wisdom and support for those around them and in a relationship they thrive on feeling needed. If the ENFJ's partner refuses to open up and share their struggles with the ENFJ, the ENFJ may feel as though they have no purpose within the partnership. And that perceived lack of purpose will be romantically unsatisfying to the ENFJ, who will likely elect to leave the relationship.

INFP: Being close-minded.

When Winona Ryder said, "I think too much. I think ahead. I think behind. I think sideways. I think it all. If it exists, I've fucking thought of it," She may as well have been describing the INFP personality. This type is obsessively open-minded and there's nothing more infuriating to them than a person who refuses to consider alternate points of view. INFPs need a deep, compelling partner who can keep up with their ever-shifting kaleidoscope of thoughts and emotions.

ENFP: Having limits placed on their freedom.

ENFPs have big visions of what they want to experience in life – and they aren't interested in discarding those visions for anyone else. Though they're happy to accommodate and incorporate a partner into their lives, the ENFP has no interest in a relationship that is going to hold them back – they need an open-minded partner who is happy to explore and adventure their way through life together.

CHAPTER 14.

THE BEST THING ABOUT DATING EACH PERSONALITY TYPE

ENTP: They are a goldmine of weird, creative ideas and you will never be bored again.

INTP: Their thoughts and emotions run deep – you will never have a shallow or uninteresting conversation again.

ENTJ: They will find a concrete way to help you achieve literally everything you've ever wanted in life.

INTJ: Their fascinating minds will make you reconsider the way that you think about everything.

ESFJ: They will make sure your every need is

met from the moment you meet until the day you die.

ISFJ: They will support you without any reservation, both practically and emotionally; from the day they meet you until the day they die.

ESFP: Their warmth and spontaneity will make each day you spend with them more exciting than the last.

ISFP: Their soulful, artistic personality will give you a new appreciation of the world that surrounds you.

ISTJ: They are loyal to the core and the ultimate providers.

ESTJ: They are tremendously committed to their relationships and fiercely protective of their loved ones.

ISTP: Their straightforward, live-for-the-moment attitude is both refreshing and compelling.

ESTP: Their spontaneity and enthusiasm will sweep you off your feet – and their straightforward attitude is endlessly refreshing.

INFJ: They will take the time to deeply understand you and will empathize with you on every level.

ENFJ: They will listen to your deepest, darkest secrets and love you even more for them.

INFP: They will love and understand you even better than you love and understand yourself.

ENFP: Their positive energy will light up your life.

CHAPTER 15.

WHAT EACH MYERS-BRIGGS PERSONALITY TYPE DOES AFTER A BREAKUP

ENTP – Takes FULL ADVANTAGE OF THEIR NEWFOUND FREEDOM and then gets inexplicably bummed out two months later.

INTP – Throws themselves into video games, soft drugs or pretty much anything that will interfere with them processing any sort of emotion.

ENTJ – Claims to be over it immediately but is later found yelling nonsensically at a chair.

INTJ – Rationalizes the end of the relationship and convinces themselves there was no other possible outcome than the breakup... while uncharacteristically drinking or binge-eating ice cream.

ESFJ – Rants incessantly to friends until they feel ready to throw themselves back into the 'dating game' full-force.

ISFJ – Incessantly pours over every mistake they made in the relationship, trying to pinpoint exactly what they did wrong.

ESFP – Surrounds themselves with anyone who can affirm that they're still hot, interesting and worth dating. Makes a deliberate point to do everything that being in a relationship was holding them back from.

ISFP – Disappears from the world indefinitely to listen to sad music and process their emotions.

ISTJ – Replays details of the relationship in their mind over and over again until they've reasoned their way to closure.

ESTJ – Loudly claims that it was their decision to end things, but secretly reminisces about the relationship when alone and is off-put by their own unexpectedly strong emotions.

ISTP – Detaches from their emotions and goes on an indefinite spree of sensory indulgence.

ESTP – Throws themselves into meeting new people and indulging in new experiences as an attempt to forget that the relationship ever happened at all.

INFJ – Withdraws to reconstruct their vision of the future without their ex in it, then seeks out the company of positive friends to lift their spirits.

ENFJ – Throws themselves into full-on 'future planning' mode to distract themselves from their feelings until they're ready to move on to the next relationship.

INFP – Retreats to cry and write out their feelings until they have fully processed the breakup.

ENFP – Tells everyone they're over it, puts on a sunny face and secretly dies inside.

CHAPTER 16.

WHAT EACH MYERS-BRIGGS PERSONALITY TYPE WAS LIKE AS A CHILD

ENTP: The troublemaker child who was constantly pushing the teacher's boundaries to see which rules could be bent.

INTP: The spacey child who accidentally walked into things a lot because he/she was busy wondering whether Martians were capable of understanding human language.

ENTJ: The child who ruled the playground through a mixture of intimidation and sophisticated political tactics.

INTJ: The reserved child who occasionally blurted out something so intelligent that their parents and teachers felt genuinely intimidated.

ESFJ: The popular child who dictated the rules of the playground by selectively handing out friendship necklaces.

ISFJ: The sweet, well-mannered child whom all the other parents kind of wished was their child.

ESFP: The class clown who considered no stunt too dangerous if it would temporarily earn them the spotlight.

ISFP: The easy-going child who always volunteered to go along with whatever game or activity would make their friends the happiest.

ISTJ: The obedient child who took their chores and corresponding allowance more seriously than most adults take their full-time jobs.

ESTJ: The schoolyard bully, who genuinely thought he was doing everyone a favor by telling them what was wrong with them.

ISTP: The child whose LEGO skills were matched only by educated architects.

ESTP: The daredevil child who got themselves banned from most of the playground equipment by second grade.

INFJ: The 'old soul' child who acted like more of an adult than their parents.

ENFJ: The child whom everyone in their class referred to as their best friend.

INFP: The people-pleasing child who consistently put on a happy face at school, then came home and cried about something a classmate said to them six hours before.

ENFP: The wildly imaginative child who had ten thousand different answers to the question "What do you want to be when you grow up?"

CHAPTER 17.

HERE'S WHO YOU WERE IN HIGH SCHOOL BASED ON YOUR PERSONALITY TYPE

ENTP

You were the hot nerd. You could usually be found arguing with teachers and authority figures over the latest lesson that they were wrong about, just because you felt like raising hell. You were a badass with brains and it was sexy. High school was okay but you couldn't wait to get out and have complete autonomy over your life.

INTP

You were a chill nerd. You were smart but didn't much care for the way most subjects were taught and chose to skip school quite a bit. The social scene didn't much interest you, save for a few friends who you sat with at lunch and talked Star Wars with. You pretty much just rode high school out, earning decent grades with minimal effort and frustrating teachers with your consistent refusal to 'apply yourself.'

ENTJ

You were the student body president. You kept a tight reign on your social standing, extra curricular presence and grade point average. You were neurotic but in a way that worked for you. You were voted "Most likely to become the next President" in your high school yearbook, which you oversaw the production for.

INTJ

You were a stereotypical nerd. You took advanced placement everything and consistently achieved straight As. You didn't have much time for the politics or drama of high school because you were busy preparing your application for Harvard, which you got into by the end of your junior year. High school was a largely uninteresting time for you and you regarded it only as a means to the end of higher education.

ESFJ

You were popular. High school was a place where you naturally thrived, as you enjoyed navigating the politics that came along with placing one thousand angsty teenagers together and forcing them to mingle relentlessly. You dated often, played whatever sport it was cool to play and were probably kind of mean for the first couple of years. You still miss high school a bit, to be honest.

ISFJ

You were the teacher's pet. You got straight A's, scraped by socially and ended up marrying your high school sweetheart. You were too sweet to be picked on but too shy to be popular so you stuck close to a few good friends and just rode your teen years out.

ESFP

You held all of the parties worth going to in high school. You were effortlessly popular and widely desired by the opposite sex. You had a natural knack for athleticism, fashion and charming others, which allowed you to be dominant without engaging in the deadly sin of trying too hard. Everyone wanted to be you or be on you and high school was a time that you enjoyed.

ISFP

You were the quiet, artistic kid with awesome taste in music. Social status wasn't your greatest concern but you were just alternative enough to be considered cool and got invited to all the right parties. You were known for always bringing a blunt and for being surprisingly insightful.

ISTJ

You were probably the hall monitor. Sticking to the rules was your jam and you consistently achieved straight A's through hard work, dedication and diligence. Once you memorized basic social protocol you got on okay with your peers but never cared to get too involved in the social scene. You were over high school by your sophomore year and couldn't wait to be around levelheaded adults in the real world.

ESTJ

You were the high school bully. You quickly picked up on social protocols and rose to the top of the food chain because others feared your wrath. You were a somewhat obnoxious teenager who could usually be found taking lunch money off the emo kids or picking a fight to flex your muscles.

ISTP

You were the skater boy Avril Lavigne was singing about. You were punk back when punk was a thing and your attitude of genuine aloofness was attractive to the opposite sex (Unfortunately you were too aloof to notice). You thought high school was, in a word, meh.

But that was your opinion on everything.

ESTP

You were a jock. You were the first of your friends to get laid and you enjoyed the sense of superiority it brought you. You popped your collar, played a lot of sports and possibly dealt a few drugs on the side. Teachers liked you so you skimmed by in school. High school was a good time for you.

INFJ

You were a band geek. Your best friends were fellow band geeks, one of whom you lost your virginity to and then dated on and off until high school ended. You got straight A's, but that was a given. When you were not in band practice you could be found reading alone in the library, wearing an "I <3 Nerds" t-shirt and eyeing up the hot ENTP.

ENFJ

You were the valedictorian. You were well-liked, high-achieving, head of several social committees and you probably planned prom. You were the person everyone else's moms asked them why they couldn't be more like.

INFP

You were a bookworm. You could be found on the fringes of the social scene, hanging out with emo or hipster kids and daydreaming through most of your classes. You weren't a huge fan of high school because it didn't provide you with ample opportunity to express yourself. You knew that once you got into the real world it'd be your chance to shine.

ENFP

You were either the class clown or the drama geek, possibly both. You had a strange, disjointed friend group that ranged from total nerds to reigning socialites and mostly you just floated around. You couldn't wait to finish high school and go do your gap year in Zimbabwe, which you talked about pretty unceasingly.

CHAPTER 18.

WHAT EACH MYERS-BRIGGS TYPE DOES IN COLLEGE

ENTP: Goes to lectures for classes they're not even in and plays devil's advocate to everything the professor says, just for fun.

INTP: Lands a job as a lab assistant in their first year and is not seen outside of said lab until fifteen years later when they graduate with a PhD or three.

ENTJ: Is only in school as a formality – they've already lined up several competitive post-graduation job offers.

INTJ: Does all the required reading for the upcoming year over summer break and spends the remainder of the school year feeling vaguely annoyed with his or her classmates who just cannot seem to keep up.

ESFJ: Sits in the front of every lecture hall, color-coding their notes using various highlighters and reminding you how much you don't have your life together.

ISFJ: Spends four years taking care of their drunken roommates. Starts dating the person they'll eventually marry by the end of freshman year.

ESFP: Probably coined the phrase, "Work hard, play hard" during their college years. Emphasis on the play hard.

ISFP: Does a lot of drugs but nonetheless ends up landing a job in a creative field, earning more money than many of their high-achieving classmates.

ISTJ: Borders on a heart attack every time an assignment is handed back without adequate explanation as to exactly why they didn't achieve a higher mark.

ESTJ: Is that student at the front of the lecture hall who puts up their hand and answers a question that nobody asked, just to show that they did all the readings.

ISTP: Manages to completely flip their sleep schedule by the end of freshman year and is not seen in broad daylight again until graduation day.

ESTP: Attends class for the sole purpose of maintaining their sports scholarship and/or fraternity presidency.

INFJ: Is consistently torn between their desire to earn straight As and their desire to lament over their latest existential crisis.

ENFJ: Somehow gets straight 90s while also running several campus clubs and maintaining a serious relationship.

INFP: Is enthralled to finally leave their small, conservative town and befriend other social justice enthusiasts whom they probably already know from tumblr.

ENFP: Starts writing every essay at 5pm the day before it's due and has still written nothing at 3am after cleaning their room, calling their mother, having a dance party, booking a spontaneous trip for spring break and composing several inspired blog articles.

CHAPTER 19.

WHAT EACH PERSONALITY TYPE IS LIKE AS AN EMPLOYEE

ENTP: The employee who comes up with a (self-proclaimed) brilliant new way of doing things every two to three days, which he or she then tries to force the rest of the reluctant office to get on board with.

INTP: The employee who holes up in his or her office all day mumbling vaguely about leaving to pursue self-employment – but never actually goes anywhere.

ENTJ: The employee who is inexplicably making four times more money than everyone else who is working the exact same job as them.

INTJ: The employee who is constantly

submitting complaints to the HR department about the inefficient nature of shutting down the office early every second Friday to attend the ESFP's beloved "Office Karaoke Night."

ESFJ: The cheerful employee who regularly brings in coffee and homemade treats for everyone to share. Doubles as the most reliable source for office gossip.

ISFJ: The incredibly sweet, hardworking employee who deals with all work-place conflicts by leaving passive-aggressive post-it notes by the copy machine.

ESFP: The employee who organizes regular office get-togethers that almost always involve karaoke and booze.

ISFP: The employee who quietly defies any sort of micromanagement by adding an unexpected creative flare to every project they're given.

ISTJ: The dutiful employee who shows up half an hour early each morning and keeps a detailed list of all the ways in which the other employees aren't following the official workplace procedures to a T.

ESTJ: The employee who applied for their boss's position one week into working there (and every consecutive week since).

ISTP: Either the official IT department or the unofficial IT department. Best known by other workers as the employee who has won the fantasy football league for ten consecutive years.

ESTP: The smooth-talking office heartthrob, who can inexplicably sooth any outraged client instantly.

INFJ: The employee everyone tells their grievances to, despite the fact that they hate dealing with everyone's grievances and wishes they'd all just work it out with each other.

ENFJ: Either the official HR director or the unofficial HR director. Spends the majority of their time at work making sure everyone else is feeling safe, happy and respected.

INFP: The one who always shows up fifteen minutes late, but nonetheless takes their devotion to the company as seriously as they take their own lives.

ENFP: The employee who spends half of their day working furiously to complete something they forgot about by its 12:00 deadline and the other half of the day giving the other employees unwarranted inspirational pep talks.

CHAPTER 20.

WHAT EACH MYERS-BRIGGS TYPE DOES WHEN THEY'RE SICK

ENTP – Develops a plethora of strange new medicines that they test on themselves, ultimately extending their sickness weeks longer than necessary.

INTP – Googles ten thousand variations of what they might have and ends up in the depths of Wikipedia, learning about a strange Polynesian virus that died out 1000 years ago.

ENTJ – Rests for about 30 minutes, decides that's enough self-care and then gets the hell back to work.

INTJ – Pops some drugs, ignores their sickness and grows steadily more annoyed each time someone asks them how they're feeling.

ESFJ – Tries to get better as quickly as possible so that they can take care of any friends or loved ones who have also caught their bug.

ISFJ – Tries to convince everyone that they're fine, really, they don't need any help... while secretly wishing that one of their loved ones would ignore their pleas and come take care of them.

ESFP – Texts all their friends that they're DYING, who wants to come over for a movie night?

ISFP – Secretly revels in having a socially acceptable excuse to stay home and do their own thing for a week or so.

ISTJ – Sticks determinately to whatever methods of getting better they were taught as a child, because that's what has always worked for them, so why switch it up?

ESTJ – Works fervently from bed on their laptop while internally scolding their immune system for not trying harder.

ISTP – Takes enough medication to get a little high and then relishes in the excuse to stay home and play video games.

ESTP – Pops some drugs, chugs an energy drink and goes about their business as usual. If it's not terminal, what's there to complain about?

INFJ – Avoids medication unless they absolutely HAVE to take it, but stays home to rest and recoup. No way are they going to let others see them in a vulnerable state!

ENFJ – Maintains their commitments with a sunny face – not wanting to burden other people with their sickness – and then goes home and crashes hard.

INFP – Stays home and fantasizes (in a totally non-morbid way, of course) about all the nice things people would say about them at their funeral.

ENFP – Refuses to rest or relax – disbelieving that this will help them get better – and goes about their day as usual, getting everyone they encounter sick in the process.

CHAPTER 21.

WHAT EACH MYERS-BRIGGS TYPE DOES ON VACATION

ENTP: Somehow learns the local language in less than a week and charms their way into everything for free.

INTP: Embarks on a solitary road trip with no fixed destination.

ENTJ: Calculates (and enforces) the precise amount of time that ought to be spent at each tourist attraction, based on an algorithm that compares utiles of happiness to time spent admiring beautiful landmarks.

INTJ: Selects the optimal hotel, dining and entertainment options by methodically narrowing down a list of possible selections prior to the trip.

ESFJ: Makes sure everyone's wearing sunscreen and wakes up early each morning to pack the group lunch.

ISFJ: Thoughtfully selects souvenirs for loved ones back home and mementos to put in their scrapbook.

ESFP: Has a whirlwind vacation romance.

ISFP: Sees a great photo op, wanders into a back alley to capture the perfect lighting and gets lost. Rejoins the group three days later.

ISTJ: Schedules visits to every museum and historical site within a hundred mile radius.

ESTJ: Manages the trip budget.

ISTP: Stays home and enjoys the solitude of everyone being gone at last.

ESTP: Convinces everyone to go bungee jumping.

INFJ: Spends vacation volunteering on a local organic farm.

ENFJ: Spends the trip resolving group

conflicts and ensuring that their travel companions are enjoying themselves.

INFP: Hopes no one notices that they snuck away to a secluded beach to read.

ENFP: Wants to dine, live and mingle like the locals in order to have the most authentic experience possible.

CHAPTER 22.

WHAT EACH MYERS-BRIGGS TYPE IS SECRETLY SMUG ABOUT

ENTP: Having to do half the work to achieve twice the success of others, because they're sharper and more creative than the other types.

INTP: Having a more accurate and objective world-view than everyone else who is so easily swayed by social trends and the garbage that the media feeds them.

ENTJ: Naturally assuming every position of leadership because they're obviously more intelligent and driven than the other types.

INTJ: Understanding all of the deepest, most intimate truths about how the world works but not sharing those truths, because the commoners wouldn't understand.

ESFJ: Being popular and socially dominant because they're more in tune with the rules of social conduct than the other types.

ISFJ: Being more genuinely selfless than the other types, because they don't call any attention to their altruistic nature.

ESFP: Being hotter and more socially savvy than the other types, without even having to try.

ISFP: Being a big, creative mystery to the other types, because they don't deserve to understand the ISFP's true self.

ISTJ: Being more principled than the other types in literally everything they do.

ESTJ: Understanding the clearest and most obvious route to success that the other types somehow missed, even though it's right there for everyone to see.

ISTP: Seeing the shortcuts for getting things done that the other types don't see because they're too busy learning the rules to actually pay attention to how things work.

ESTP: Understanding how to get things done without following the bullshit rules and procedures that the rest of the other types are obsessed with.

INFJ: Understanding everyone they meet but nobody understanding them, because they're rarer and more complex than the other types.

ENFJ: Knowing what's best for everyone, because they're wiser and more emotionally savvy than the other types.

INFP: Being profoundly misunderstood by everyone else because they're deeper and more interesting than the other types.

ENFP: Leading an unconventional life because they're more daring and creative than the other types.

CHAPTER 23.

WHAT EACH MYERS-BRIGGS TYPE DOES WHEN THEY'RE ANGRY (AND WHAT THEY SHOULD DO INSTEAD)

ENTP:

What they do: Attacks the other person's deepest weaknesses and insecurities, either through a series of subtle insults or all at once in a fit of blind rage.

What they ought to do instead: Consider what role they played in the situation and then explain their point of view to the opposing party and ask for theirs.

INTP:

What they do: Ignores their anger for years at a

time until they eventually snap unexpectedly and spew snarky insults about the opposing party's intelligence.

What they ought to do instead: Take note of when and why they're feeling angry, rather than pushing it down, in order to avoid outbursts.

ENTJ:

What they do: Turns cold and calculating, then takes down the opposing party's argument with a single well-timed phrase or action that gets the ENTJ their way.

What they ought to do: Withdraw to process their feelings on the conflict rather than immediately strategizing a way to 'win' it.

INTJ:

What they do: Decides the person they're mad at is incompetent and ices them out.

What they ought to do instead: Let the other person know that they've upset them but that they'd like to hear their side of the situation and to determine a solution to the conflict.

ESFJ:

What they do: Forgives the indiscretion in the moment but then never, ever forgets about it.

What they ought to do: Learn to process feelings of hurt and betrayal as they occur, in order to let them go and move on from past hurts.

ISFJ:

What they do: Holds their anger in, convincing themselves that they can just get over it, but then lets it out subtly, in passive-aggressive bouts.

What they ought to do instead: Communicate their hurt to the opposite party and brainstorm ways to avoid repeating it in the future.

ESFP:

What they do: Yells, cries and makes a scene – and then de-escalates quickly and apologizes.

What they ought to do instead: Take a moment to consider how they ought to best communicate their point of view – and then calmly let the opposing party know that their feelings have been hurt.

ISFP:

What they do: Holds in their anger and avoids the person they're mad at, possibly for the rest of their lives.

What they ought to do instead: Explain to the opposing party why their feelings were hurt and then ask to hear their side of the situation.

ISTJ:

What they do: Oscillates between ignoring the person they're angry with and directing subtle yet cruel/belittling comments their way.

What they ought to do instead: Ask the person

they're upset with to explain their point of view – and then share their own in a non-confrontational manner.

ESTJ:

What they do: Impatiently barks orders at others and shames them for their way of doing things.

What they ought to do: Consider how their reaction to a stressful situation may impact their relationship with those around them and come up with a more effective measure of communicating when under stress.

ISTP:

What they do: Ignores the actual person they're mad at and engages in a sensory experience that takes their mind off the issue (I.e. Drinking, fighting, exercising).

What they ought to do instead: Find a healthy physical outlet for their anger (I.e. exercise) and then find a solution to the problem that initially angered them.

ESTP:

What they do: Feels an intense physical reaction and lets it out by confronting others and/or punching/smashing an inanimate object.

What they ought to do: Find a constructive release for their physical energy (I.e. exercising or meditating) so that they can take a step back from their anger and focus on the problem itself.

INFJ:

What they do: If slightly angered, retreats and ices out the opposing party. If deeply angered (this is rare), will use every one of the other person's weaknesses against them until they have completely psychologically undermined them.

What they ought to do instead: Communicate openly with the person they are angry with in order to find a solution, rather than letting it reach a breaking point.

ENFJ:

What they do: If slightly angered, retreats to analyze the situation. If greatly angered, attacks the opposing party with cruel personal truths about him or her.

What they ought to do instead: Recognize the subjective nature of their anger and keep an open mind to the opposite party's point of view while discussing the issue.

INFP:

What they do: Retreats to analyze the situation and determine whether or not they are overreacting. May give the silent treatment to the person they are upset with in the meantime.

What they ought to do instead: Before retreating, tell the person they are upset with that their feelings have been hurt and that they require some alone time to process the situation.

ENFP:

What they do: Attempts to look at things from

the other person's point of view and if it's not what the ENFP would do, shames the other person for their way of handling the situation.

What they ought to do instead: Ask the other person to explain their side of the situation and try to understand the intent behind their actions.

CHAPTER 24.

HERE'S WHICH BRATTY BEHAVIOR EACH PERSONALITY TYPE NEEDS TO CHECK THEMSELVES FOR

ENTP: Taking advantage of people.

ENTPs have a knack for quickly picking up on just what makes people tick. And in the unhealthy or underdeveloped ENTP, that knack can take a quick turn for the manipulative. This type knows exactly how to push peoples buttons to get what they want out of them – and they often aren't concerned with how the situation plays out for the person they're taking advantage of. This type needs to learn to reign in their manipulative tendencies before their bad behavior blows up in their face.

INTP: Neglecting loved ones.

INTPs live predominantly inside their own minds. This type requires less social stimulation than almost any other type, and an unhealthy INTP may cope by shutting out other people altogether. INTPs need to ensure that during times of trouble, they aren't failing to appreciate the people who stick by them. Their loved ones may feel neglected by their reclusiveness, interpreting it as a lack of investment in the relationship.

ENTJ: Coercing others into submission.

ENTJs are powerhouses. They are masters of pinpointing the most efficient way of getting things done – and occasionally, those ways of getting things done require the participation of other people. While a healthy ENTJ maintains and respects others' boundaries, an unhealthy one may cash in on their manipulative tendencies and coerce others into acting in a way that serves them. This type tends to believe that the ends justify the means – which is effective in the best of times but morally questionable in the worst of times.

INTJ: Assuming they have nothing to learn from others.

INTJs are incredibly knowledgeable – and they know it. Unhealthy versions of this type are prone to narcissistic tendencies, and may altogether refuse to listen to what anyone around them has to say – assuming themselves to be the only competent individual around. This type needs to remember that there are different forms of intelligence and they don't possess them all. Chances are, they have a great deal to learn from those around them – even those they initially deem incompetent.

ESFJ: Gossiping.

ESFJs are interested in what people are doing. And unhealthy ESFJs are interested in judging what people are doing. No matter how juicy a particular piece of gossip may be, ESFJs have to learn when it's simply time to bite their tongues. Many unhealthy ESFJs develop reputations for being warm in person but judgmental behind their friends' backs – and that's a reputation nobody wants.

ISFJ: Unwarranted passive-aggressiveness.

ISFJs like to make others happy – and for that reason, they often feel uncomfortable expressing their own needs. Unhealthy ISFJs may harbor grudges against friends or acquaintances for years – feeling bitter about their needs going unmet, despite the fact that they never explicitly voiced them. This type needs to remember that their loved ones are not mind readers and that their passive-aggressiveness isn't warranted until they've actually raised their concerns.

ESFP: Chasing the spotlight at all costs.

ESFPs love to be the center of attention. This type thrives on entertaining others – and there's nothing wrong with that! But an unhealthy ESFP is at risk of neglecting loyal friends and loved ones every time an opportunity for attention arises. They may flake on plans, drop commitments and even fail to be there for friends in times of need if they perceive a greater opportunity for validation. This type needs to remember that attention is fleeting but long-lasting relationships are not.

ISFP: Avoiding necessary confrontation.

Healthy ISFPs know that as much as they dislike confrontation, it's occasionally necessary to iron out conflicts that arise within a relationship. Unhealthy ISFPs, on the other hand, would rather throw out the entire relationship than let someone know that something they did offended them. ISFPs need to keep in mind that sometimes ironing out conflicts is a necessary evil – and that avoiding confrontation often only aggravates a situation.

ISTJ: Assuming moral superiority.

ISTJs are incredibly principled individuals – they take their duties and commitments incredibly seriously and appreciate when others do as well. In unhealthy ISTJs, however, this sense of duty can manifest as a moral superiority complex – the ISTJ may decide that others are morally corrupt and fail to understand that their own system of morality differs from those of others. This type needs to keep in mind that their own version of right and wrong is the only one they have control over!

ESTJ: Lecturing others.

If ESTJs are anything, it's self-assured. This type is confident in their worldview and tends to genuinely believe that they know what's best for those around them – but that isn't always the case. Unhealthy ESTJs lack the ability to recognize that their worldview doesn't always translate for others – and that they have to be tolerant of other people's choices, regardless of how illogical they may seem to them.

ISTP: Unwarranted grouchiness.

ISTPs need a lot of time to process things internally. And if that time gets interrupted, unhealthy ISTPs have the tendency to respond grouchily towards whoever interrupted their train of thought – even if they did so entirely innocently. This type needs to remember that it wouldn't kill them to fake social pleasantries from time to time, even if they're not really in the mood.

ESTP: Playing people to get what they want.

ESTPs are smooth talkers and charmers. They can talk their way in or out of anything and an unhealthy ESTP may take advantage of this ability. This type needs to remember that they're accountable for everything they say while their charm is turned on – and that if they make a promise in order to get something they want, they're still accountable for delivering on it.

INFJ: Pretentiousness.

INFJs are a generally misunderstood personality type – they make up less than 1% of the population and aren't easy to get to know well. And unhealthy INFJs are thoroughly pleased with being misunderstood. They may use their uncommon nature as a means of belittling others for lacking their depth or analytical abilities, or as an excuse for looking down on the more common types. INFJs need to remember that rare is not synonymous with superior, and that every type is fundamentally misunderstood in some way.

ENFJ: Interfering with people's personal lives.

ENFJs want nothing more than to help their friends make the choices that are best for them. And unhealthy ENFJs often do so by manipulating their friends to make the choice they believe to be right – regardless of what their friend wants. ENFJs need to remember that as emotionally intelligent as they may be, they need to let others make their own decisions. Getting caught meddling puts them at risk of losing the trust of their loved ones and making the entire situation worse than ever.

INFP: Holding others to unrealistic expectations.

INFPs almost always see the best in people. And unhealthy INFPs invent the best in people. This wildly imaginative type is occasionally guilty of embellishing someone in their imagination to the point where they become upset with the real-life version of said person for not living up to their imaginary ideal. This type needs to keep in mind that their fantasies don't always match up to reality – and that sometimes they're expectations for others can be a wee bit unrealistic.

ENFP: Disappearing on people.

ENFPs have a lot of feelings but a short attention span – which means their feelings for other people tend to change quickly. Unhealthy ENFPs have the tendency to keep their options open at the expense of other people – they may string friends or love interests along while they consider their many options for romance or the future in general. And as soon as something new catches their eye, they are at risk of disappearing without warning and leaving a string of confused loved ones in their wake.

CHAPTER 25.

HOW EACH MYERS-BRIGGS PERSONALITY TYPE PREPARES FOR THE HOLIDAYS

ENTP – Trolls Internet forums pretending to be deeply offended about various holiday-related issues that they actually couldn't care less about.

INTP – Breaks out in a cold sweat at the thought of all the holiday parties they're about to be expected to attend.

ENTJ – Capitalizes on the holiday season by designing their company's advertising campaign around the spirit of giving.

INTJ – Attempts to explain the inefficiency of gift swapping to their family but ends up reluctantly sporting their Mother's annual holiday scarf while they hand out gift cards.

ESFJ – Starts viciously baking and freezing treats two months ahead of time. Nearly explodes with excitement planning their holiday party.

ISFJ – Settles down to watch their favorite holiday specials that they've been enjoying every year since childhood.

ESFP – Spikes the eggnog and hangs the mistletoe at every holiday party they attend.

ISFP – Goes shopping for cute, vintage holiday sweaters to sport before the best things get picked over when 'ugly sweater party' season begins.

ISTJ – Begins subtly asking their loved ones what they need in the way of household or personal items, in order to determine the most practical gift they can get for them.

ESTJ – Adheres to whichever holiday traditions are most important to their family, but spends the entire time making mental to-do lists for work the next day.

ISTP – Pops popcorn and sits back to watch what everyone's going to be offended by this year.

ESTP – Loudly wishes everyone at work a "Merry Christmas" instead of a "Happy Holidays" and is called in for sensitivity training.

INFJ – Drives themselves crazy trying to narrow down the MOST PERFECT gift for everyone, that is in equal parts meaningful and practical.

ENFJ – Sees the holiday season as one big opportunity to bring their loved ones together and begins planning various themed celebrations.

INFP – Channels the holiday spirit to help them up the ante on the 'random acts of kindness' that they already regularly engage in.

ENFP – Gets so excited about the holiday festivities that they completely forget to go gift shopping and end up ferociously wrapping presents at 11pm on Christmas Eve.

CHAPTER 26.

HERE IS WHAT HAPPENS WHEN EACH MYERS-BRIGGS PERSONALITY TYPE MAKES A NEW YEAR'S RESOLUTION

ENTP

"I resolve to only turn every second conversation into a heated dispute."

Outcome: Finds an unsuspecting ESFJ to debate the practicality of this resolution with.

INTP

"I resolve to find practical implications for my work since the physical world does, unfortunately, exist."

Outcome: Derives a theoretical implication for the practicality of their latest project and considers their resolution a success.

ENTJ

"I resolve to screw over marginally less of my colleagues as I fearlessly charge towards success."

Outcome: Keeps a detailed chart of co-workers they are not preying on. Eventually hires a colleague to manage this chart as a distraction while the ENTJ rises above them professionally.

INTJ

"I resolve to listen to the opinions of my less intelligent underlings."

Outcome: Derives motivation from the opinions of commoners to fuel a series of research projects that prove everyone's opinions to be indisputably wrong.

ESFJ

"I resolve to gossip less and accept others' choices without judgment."

Outcome: Phones their closest friend to ask what their resolution is and then phones fourteen of their *other* closest friends to discuss their first friend's resolution in totally non-judgmental detail.

ISFJ

"I resolve to spend more time focusing on what I want instead of catering to the needs of others."

Outcome: Mercilessly commits to this resolution until a loved one implies that it is inconveniencing them.

ESFP

"I resolve to party less... On weeknights... Before 5pm."

Outcome: Drunkenly announces their resolution to five hundred of their closest friend on Thursday January 1st, at the bar, at 4pm.

ISFP

"I resolve to give myself more credit for my talents and advocate for my own abilities."

Outcome: Sits down to review their strengths, decides on twelve new ways in which their art form is imperfect and gets back to working on perfecting it.

ISTJ

"I resolve to be less regimented and spend more time relaxing."

Outcome: Schedules relaxation between 3:15 and 3:42pm each afternoon, during which time they create detailed lists of how they will relax on following days.

ESTJ

"I resolve to find subtler ways of letting everyone know that my way is always best."

Outcome: Loudly announces to colleagues that they all ought to make the same New Years resolution.

ISTP

"I resolve to get serious about one of my side interests and turn it into a profitable enterprise."

Outcome: Develops a keen side interest in entrepreneurship, which they thoroughly analyze and develop ideas about.

ESTP

"I resolve to think through the consequences of my actions before I make them."

Outcome: Adheres to their resolution for the first two – four days before being presented with a better plan and impulsively getting on board with that one instead.

INFJ

"I resolve to be less of a perfectionist and share more of myself with others."

Outcome: Refuses to disclose resolution to others, for fear that they will have to admit failure if they do not achieve it.

ENFJ

"I resolve to avoid meddling in the lives of my loved ones, even if they are making a mistake."

Outcome: Allows their friends to fail at their new years resolutions, then sits each of them down to talk about what went wrong and how they can fix it.

INFP

I resolve to stop falling in love with the idea of people and being disappointed when their reality does not match up.

Outcome: Explains this resolution in a heartfelt letter to their love interest, who they just know will understand.

ENFP

"I resolve to make less than thirty new years

resolutions this year, and keep at least two of them."

Outcome: Stays up for fourteen straight days in an attempt to complete first resolution and subsequently ends up creating fifteen more.

CHAPTER 27.

HERE'S WHAT EACH TYPE NEEDS ON A BAD DAY

ENTP: A stimulating conversation that helps them generate new theories or ideas.

INTP: A new project to distract them from self-destructive thoughts.

ENTJ: To form a concrete, detailed plan for improving the situation that has gotten them down.

INTJ: A good book and the day to themselves to re-charge.

ESFJ: To be told they're appreciated by the people they're closest to. And/or to be pampered a little!

ISFJ: To have little favours done for them, as a reminder that they are allowed to relax.

ESFP: Lots of human interaction and praise.

ISFP: Patience with their mood (they need to work themselves through it) and perhaps a fun physical distraction.

ISTJ: Alternate solutions to the problem they're facing and the knowledge that they can rely on you if they need help.

ESTJ: For someone to ask them what they can do to help. They probably know the answer.

ISTP: To be presented with a few fun options to take if he/she wants them, and then to be left alone.

ESTP: To do something rambunctious and physical with friends that will re-energize them to power through whatever situation is troubling them.

INFJ: A good long laugh with a friend they can be silly with and possibly some time outdoors/in nature.

ENFJ: A huge hug and a sincere reminder of

why you love them and all that you've learned from them.

INFP: To be listened to with patience and to have their feelings validated.

ENFP: To brainstorm fun possibilities and/or plan an adventure.

CHAPTER 28.

HERE IS WHAT EACH
PERSONALITY TYPE IS AFRAID OF

ENTP: Limitations

ENTPs are explorers, inventors and boundary-pushers. The scariest thing this type can think of is having hard and fast limitations placed on their behavior. When an ENTP wants something, nothing can hold them back from going after it – and the thought of anything that could gives them the heebie-jeebies.

INTP: Ignorance

INTPs need to look at a given situation from every possible angle before they can properly understand it – and to them, it is truly terrifying to conceive of a world in which others refuse to do the same. The effects of ignorance are monstrously apparent to the INTP – they shudder to think of what would happen if the truly ignorant people of the world were regularly put into power.

ENTJ: Powerlessness

ENTJs are born leaders. This type maintains a clear vision of what they want at all times and the idea of being powerless to take control of their lives is terrifying to them. An ENTJ without an action plan is a fish out of water. And it's a damn scary thought.

INTJ: Being In The Dark Intellectually

INTJs aim to develop a comprehensive understanding of the world around them – and in order to do so, they need to learn as much about it as they possibly can. This highly intellectual type prides themselves on having a thorough knowledge of anything that interests them – and the idea of being held back from learning, in any capacity, is genuinely scary to them.

ESFJ: Isolation

ESFJs live to serve their loved ones. This endlessly personable type derives energy from those around them and they top the charts as one of the most extroverted personality types. Being isolated or disconnected from others drives an ESFJ mad – and being genuinely alone in life is a truly fearful thought to them.

ISFJ: A Disruption Of The Peace

ISFJs thrive in calm, cooperative environments where everything runs as it should and everyone gets along cordially. This type loathes the idea of having their peaceful world disturbed in an unresolvable way. Experiencing conflicting desires, interpersonal disagreements or any other disruption of harmony is their ultimate fear.

ESFP: Disinterest From Others

ESFPs live to perform, entertain and excite those around them. The spotlight is where they thrive and their idea of horror is a world in which nobody finds them interesting or entertaining. They live to explore people possibilities and the idea of those possibilities disappearing truly scares them.

ISFP: Rigidity

ISFPs crave the freedom to express themselves like the rest of us crave water and air. This type needs to go out into the world and explore, discover and create without limitations, in order to feel like themselves. A rigid, stifling environment is terrifying to this type. They fear having their self-expression limited in any way.

ISTJ: Lawlessness

ISTJs are the ultimate rule-abiders – and a word without rules is perhaps the most terrifying thing they can think of. This type wishes to instill order upon every area of their lives and without a system of organization they are lost. A lawless world is a truly horrifying idea to this type.

ESTJ: Submission

ESTJs like to be at large and in charge – and the idea of having to submit to those less competent terrifies them. Though they can certainly take orders from people they respect, ESTJs crave power and control over their circumstances – and the idea of being at someone else's will drives them mad.

ISTP: Hands-Off Learning

The ISTP lives to understand the world in a direct, concrete fashion. They learn by tinkering, testing, experimenting and meddling. A world in which they are expected to blindly accept how things work is a world that they don't want to live in. The ISTP needs to get their hands dirty in life – and being held back from doing so is a truly terrifying thought.

ESTP: A Lack Of Self-Sufficiency

ESTPs are the ultimate doers –they see a clear path between to what they want and they won't stand for anything getting in their way.

The ESTP's worst nightmare is being unable to provide for him or her self. They are independent to a fault and having their self-sufficiency compromised is a downright terrifying thought.

INFJ: Corruption

The INFJ has a unique understanding of how humans relate to one another on a large scale – and because of this, there is perhaps nothing they fear more than our large-scale ability to hurt, cheat and take advantage of one another. They understand how these actions negatively affect us all – and as a result, they are abhorrent of our capacity to take part in them.

ENFJ: Unresolvable conflict

ENFJs are the masters of smoothing over conflict between people they love – and the idea of not being able to do so strikes fear into their hearts. Without their magical interpersonal communication skills, the ENFJ would feel useless to those around them. And there's no thought more terrifying to this type than being useless to those they love.

INFP: Oppression

INFPs believe fiercely in equal rights and freedom of thought and speech. There is nothing scarier to this open-minded type than a world in which people are not intrinsically valued, or are held back from expressing their true selves.

ENFP: Monotony

ENFPs are the ultimate novelty-seekers. These highly enthusiastic individuals want to dive headfirst into life and experience it in as many different fashions and facets as possible. The thought of getting stuck in a monotonous routine or situation is paralyzing to them. They can think of nothing worse than having their lives stay the same indefinitely.

CHAPTER 29.

HERE IS YOUR MENTAL AGE, BASED ON YOUR MYERS-BRIGGS PERSONALITY TYPE

ENTP – 24

You have the innovative spirit of an idealistic child mixed with the professional savviness of an assertive adult – landing you squarely in the 'young adult' age bracket, mentally. No matter how old you get, you retain the adventurous, opportunistic nature of someone much younger than yourself, combined with the resourceful capability of someone much older.

INTP – 45

Of all the types, INTPs may be the most

difficult to fit into a particular mental age. This type has the intellectual capacity and decisiveness of someone much older than themselves combined with the insatiable curiosity of a very young child. This type may best be described as "45 going on 3." Their unique way of perceiving the world renders them ageless in many ways – they may be totally inept at 'adulting' but intellectually gifted from a young age.

ENTJ – 55

The age of the average Fortune 500 CEO is 55 so it seemed only natural that this age would suit you best. For the majority of your life you've possessed the confidence, diligence and decisiveness of someone much older than yourself – and by middle age your body will finally catch up with the maturity of your mind. 55 may just be your time to shine... but who are we kidding. Your whole life is your time to shine.

INTJ – 80

INTJs seem to mentally age at twice the rate

of most other types. Their lifelong quest for knowledge means they advance intellectually in leaps and bounds – they have little patience for the constraints of youth and tend to befriend adults from the time they are young. This type has the wisdom of an old soul and the unconquerable thirst for knowledge that keeps them growing and expanding well beyond their years.

ESFJ – 30

You're bubbly, energetic and lively but also mature, responsible and organized – embodying all the qualities of someone who has grown confidently into young adulthood. They say our early thirties are our prime years – when we are old enough to have established ourselves, yet young enough to enjoy good health. And if you're anything, it's confident and established. You've always possessed the focus and maturity of a true adult, with the warmth and energy of someone much younger.

ISFJ – 65

You've always felt a little out of sorts around people your own age – like some part of you would rather be at home, baking cookies with your cat, than out at a wild rager. You were born with the mentality of a calm, collected adult and it hasn't wavered much over the years. You know old age will be your time to shine. You'll be the best gran or grandpa on the block.

ESFP – 16

It's not that you lack the maturity or depth of your true biological age – it's just that you embody the enthusiastic spirit of someone much younger than yourself. You are ceaselessly open to life in every facet. You work hard, play hard, love hard and live hard. Regardless of how old you become, you maintain the effervescent energy of someone much younger than yourself and it's refreshing to everyone around you.

ISFP – 23

They say your early to mid twenties are your peak creative years – but for you, your entire life is your peak creative years. Possessing the insight of someone much older than yourself but the youthful creative energy of someone much younger, your age might best be described as "23 going on 60."

ISTJ – 50

ISTJs are born responsible. This type takes their commitments direly seriously and possesses almost no trace of youthful mischievousness. They often feel older than their peers, even as children, and long to reach an age at which they will finally be taken seriously by their peers. Middle age suits the ISTJ well – they are still physically capable of getting things done, while finally being old enough to receive the respect they deserve.

ESTJ – 45

ESTJs combine the playful, gregarious spirit of a young college bro with the responsibility and diligence of a fully-formed adult. This type is obsessively professional and capable – they enjoy middle age as a time where they have earned the respect of their peers yet are still in good enough health to be able to push their own limits.

ISTP – 22

ISTPs are in their prime when they are at their physical peak – usually in their early twenties. This type has a devilishly rebellious spirit that relishes in sensory delights. And yet they do possess the capability and responsibility of a quasi-adult at any age. 22 truly does seem to suit this type, as an age at which they are able to live life on their own terms but are not yet bothered by the societal expectations of adulthood.

ESTP – 18

ESTPs are the straight-shooting rule-breakers of the world, who never fully lose their rebellious teenage spirit. This type retains the energy and enthusiasm of a young adult no matter how old they get. They won't be held back by the world around them – they get what they want when they want it and just try telling them otherwise.

INFJ – 90

Chances are, some part of you has always felt older than those around you. You dwell eternally in the deep end of life – questioning its nature and meaning in depth, while remaining endlessly patient with those around you. You have the empathy and insight of someone much older than yourself – you are a natural sage, regardless of your biological age.

ENFJ – 40

You've always naturally assumed the role of the wise mentor to those in your life. Your mental prowess resembles that of someone who is old enough to make decisions rationally and compassionately, yet young enough to execute them with an idealistic sense of enthusiasm. Your "Mother Hen" role in others' lives plants you at the beginning of middle-age, mentally. You have a youthful energy backed up by an indisputable well of wisdom.

INFP – 60

No matter what your biological age is, you were born as and remain an old soul. You have been questioning the greater truths about life for as long as you can remember, but your wisdom is supported by an inherently youthful sense of curiosity that drives you to explore each issue from multiple different angles. You may best be best described as 60 going on 6 – you have the sagacity of someone much older than yourself but the insatiable curiosity of someone much younger.

ENFP – 21

No matter how old you become, you maintain the drive, enthusiasm and passion of someone who is just coming into his or her own. You are young at heart but old in spirit – you may best be described as 21 going on 90. You have the energy of someone much younger than yourself but the wisdom of someone much older.

CHAPTER 30.

HOW EACH PERSONALITY TYPE IS LIKELY TO DIE

ENTP: An elaborate magic trick gone wrong.

INTP: Accidentally sets themselves on fire in a freak science experiment. Starts taking notes about the fire's rate of burning and consequently forgets to put it out.

ENTJ: Is elaborately murdered by an underling who wanted their job.

INTJ: Dies in a car accident caused by the fact that they were driving too cautiously.

ESFJ: Is murdered for accidentally blabbing the wrong person's secret.

ISFJ: Donates a vital organ to someone who needed it more than they did.

ESFP: Stays awake for five straight days because there were a lot of great parties going on and they had FOMO. Dies from exhaustion.

ISFP: Stages their own death to avoid confrontation with a loved one. Might still be alive out there somewhere – we'll never really know.

ISTJ: Is killed fighting for their country. Or state. Or son's little league team. Really, any cause that vaguely needs a hero to die for it.

ESTJ: Is attacked by a group of miscreant youths whom they stop to lecture on the street.

ISTP: Joins an underground Fight Club to unleash their bottled-up feelings toward 'The Man' and loses the wrong fight.

ESTP: Tries base jumping without any training because it looked straight-forward enough.

INFJ: Starves to death in a hunger strike to raise awareness about the dire state of society.

ENFJ: Meets another ENFJ and accidentally crushes each other from hugging too aggressively.

INFP: Accidentally walks into an open manhole while caught up in a particularly enthralling daydream.

ENFP: Decides to go on a "Fun Jungle Adventure!" alone, without a map, and never returns.

CHAPTER 31.

THE DEFINITION OF HELL FOR EACH MYERS-BRIGGS PERSONALITY TYPE

ENTP – Freedom of speech is revoked from the constitution. Voicing your opinion in any way is now illegal.

INTP – You are eternally condemned to researching an extremely vapid topic using wildly inaccurate methods, mostly involving interviewing people who have no idea what they're talking about.

ENTJ – Somebody is wrong, and they're directing a large group of people! You can't do anything about it and will have to obey whatever inefficient policies they decide to implement.

INTJ – Every time you open your mouth to say something intelligent, something entirely idiotic comes out instead.

ESFJ – Someone you love is in dire need of practical help and you can't give it to them. Worse yet, they think you're refusing to help them out of pettiness and they're mad at you.

ISFJ – Everyone you love is yelling at each other and it's all your fault.

ESFP – You are stuck in a room by yourself for the rest of eternity.

ISFP – You have to listen to rude people criticizing your personal choices, your appearance and your art form all day long. Nobody cares that they're hurting your feelings.

ISTJ – You are expected to complete a highly esteemed project with absolutely no guidance as to what's expected of you.

ESTJ – An incredibly impractical person is put in charge of all of your major life decisions. You have to do whatever they say and are powerless to argue or reason with them.

ISTP – The Zombie apocalypse happens but you're suddenly the world's weakest fighter and must depend solely on your loved ones to keep you alive.

ESTP – You are completely paralyzed, lacking even the ability to speak.

INFJ – You are eternally damned to working for a morally corrupt company that aims to exploit the weak and generally degrade conditions for all of society.

ENFJ – Your loved ones are in dire need of guidance but every piece of advice you gives them inadvertently makes things worse for them.

INFP – Your deepest thoughts and feelings are exposed to a large audience and everyone thinks that you're pathetic and unoriginal.

ENFP – Every minute of the rest of your life has been scheduled for you – and it's a long series of arbitrary, solitary tasks.

CHAPTER 32.

THE DEFINITION OF HEAVEN FOR EACH MYERS-BRIGGS PERSONALITY TYPE

ENTP: A world in which they have a thousand minions at their disposal to carry out any plan or invention they dream up – but of course, they get the credit for it all.

INTP: A world in which nobody is ignorant about any major issue and everybody thinks carefully before they speak.

ENTJ: A world in which they are the all-powerful rulers of everything.

INTJ: A world that automatically adapts to every new realization they have about how things ought to work, without them having to implement a thing.

ESFJ: A world without conflict, in which everyone appreciates each other's strengths and works together in harmony.

ISFJ: A world in which the health, safety and happiness of everyone they love is guaranteed.

ESFP: A world in which they're super-celebrities who can instantly date or befriend whomever they wish.

ISFP: A world in which they can earn a stable income from their creative endeavor of choice and have unlimited freedom to pursue it.

ISTJ: A world in which all the rules are followed by everyone and they are left alone to pursue their own interests.

ESTJ: A world in which they're powerful, have achieved a high social status and own a variety of expensive toys.

ISTP: A world in which they're left the hell alone to tinker with things and work on new projects.

ESTP: A world in which they're exempt from all laws and formal procedures and can directly take action on everything they want.

INFJ: A world that is devoid of corruption – in which other people finally understand and accept them.

ENFJ: A world in which everyone listens to their counsel and is infinitely happier as a result.

INFP: A world that is devoid of injustice or suffering for those who don't deserve it.

ENFP: A world in which all adventures are open to them and everyone they love is eager to come along.

CHAPTER 33.

WHAT EXHAUSTS EACH MYERS-BRIGGS PERSONALITY TYPE

ENTP – Routine

ENTPs live to alter, adjust, and improve on the mundane. This highly inventive type loves nothing more than to try out new ways of doing things – asking them to adhere to a strict routine (without altering it) is asking them to slowly drain themselves of energy. This type needs novelty the way they need water and air.

INTP – Emotional Demands

It's not that INTPs don't have emotions – it's that they have trouble accessing them on demand, and often need a great deal of time to sort through how they're feeling. If they are asked to consistently access and act upon their emotions, the INTP will quickly become drained. They need to examine a situation from absolutely all angles before they can decide what they think or feel about it. Knee-jerk emotional responses are anything but their forte.

ENTJ – Complaining

If there's anything that exhausts and frustrates an ENTJ, it's people who complain without taking action. This no-nonsense type thrives on getting things done quickly and efficiently. When the process gets held up by people who want to agonize over their feelings first and act second (or not at all), the ENTJ quickly loses energy. When held back from getting things done, this type becomes quickly frustrated.

INTJ – Improvisation

INTJs are the ultimate planners – they ruthlessly map out how they're going to behave in future situations and glean energy from determining the best of all possible approaches. Though they are capable of improvising when need be, the INTJ will rapidly lose energy if they must act without deliberating for a significant period of time. They are big-picture thinkers, and they need to put everything into perspective before they feel completely comfortable taking action.

ESFJ – Emotional Unavailability

ESFJs crave emotional connections with others. Though the 'emotionally unavailable' thing may look like a juicy challenge in the short-term, it bleeds them of energy in the long-term. This type thrives on taking care of the people they love and if they are unable to get past a cold exterior and determine what exactly that other person needs, they will feel emotionally unfulfilled and drained.

ISFJ – Inconsistent People

ISFJs thrive on nurturing and caring for their loved ones. But when the people in their lives are behaving inconsistently, it makes it difficult for the ISFJ to understand how to harmonize with them. The inability to make sense of those they love is highly stressful for the ISFJ and it rapidly drains them of energy.

ESFP – Isolation

ESFPs are all about the 'people possibilities' that exist in their external environment – they thrive on meeting and getting to know others. When robbed of the opportunity to do so, the ESFP loses energy quickly. They need to be social to be happy – isolation is their quickest path to energy loss.

ISFP – Conformity

ISFPs are the ultimate free spirits. This imaginative type likes to put their own creative spin on whatever they do, and being denied the chance to do so is exhausting for them. Being forced to conform to a uniform, no-nonsense way of doing things is suffocating for the ISFP, and will rapidly drain them of energy.

ISTJ – Unpredictable Situations

ISTJs thrive on acting in an efficient, no-nonsense manner – which means that having a well-ordered environment is crucial to them. Being in a situation that is unpredictable or disorganized is stressful for the ISTJ as it robs them of the ability to plan in a straightforward manner. Chaos and disorder is incredibly draining for this put-together type.

ESTJ – Ambiguity

ESTJs see the world in a direct, clear-cut manner. They enjoy planning and executing plans in as efficient a fashion as possible, which means they need the most applicable, concrete information available. When that information is not available – because they are in an inherently ambiguous situation – the ESTJ becomes quickly drained trying to figure out which information they should act on. They rapidly lose energy when their ability to be efficient is infringed upon.

ISTP – Neediness

ISTPs are incredibly independent creatures who require a great deal of alone time in order to thrive and gain energy. When others place excessive demands on their time and resources, the ISTP becomes quickly drained. This type needs to do things on their own time and in their own way – constantly yielding to someone else's needs wears them down quickly.

ESTP – Inaction

ESTPs are action-oriented to a fault. This type sees a direct course of action between themselves and whatever they want – and the inability to take it drives them crazy. If they are forced to reflect rather than act for an extended period of time, the ESTP becomes drained. They gain energy from doing – not from thinking about doing.

INFJ – External Conflict

INFJs are natural counselors and moderators – but that doesn't mean it is their favorite skill to practice. When this type experiences a high amount of conflict in their external environment, they feel compelled to put their energy towards resolving it. When the conflict extends for a long period of time, they will become drained by overextending themselves and will feel the intense need to withdraw. A calm, peaceful environment is what this type truly needs to thrive.

ENFJ – Impersonal Reasoning

ENFJs understand – perhaps better than any other type – that we are all connected. Asking them to take people or emotions out of a decision is borderline impossible for this type – they automatically perceive how any given situation will impact everyone involved. If they are asked to reason in an impersonal manner for an extended period of time, this type will become quickly drained. They live to help, motivate and care for those around them – not to reason them out of the picture.

INFP – Unimaginativeness

The wild imagination of the INFP is rivalled

by none – this type gains energy by taking ordinary situations and turning them into something extraordinary in their minds. Consequently, when the INFP is forced to reason in a dull, impersonal and uninventive fashion, they quickly lose energy. To this imaginative type, what could be is always more exciting than what is.

ENFP – Predictability

ENFPs thrive on the excitement of not knowing what comes next. This wildly imaginative type gains energy through speculating about the future and planning what could and might come next. Consequently, this type is drained by routine and predictability. When their options are limited and they don't have a challenge to rise to, the ENFP becomes exhausted and lifeless.

CHAPTER 34.

HOW TO MOTIVATE EACH PERSONALITY TYPE

ENTP – Tell them it can't be done.

ENTPs love a challenge – almost as much as they love proving other people wrong. The #1 way to ensure that an ENTP is going to do something is to present it to them in a way that implies you think it can't be done. They'll throw their entire beings into proving you wrong.

INTP – Tell them that everyone else is using inaccurate methods of getting it done.

INTPs are ceaselessly frustrated by the idiotic methods others use to gather and decide on information. By telling them that information is being construed incorrectly, you'll play on their major pet peeve and motivate them to show everyone else how things ought to be getting done.

ENTJ – Tell them the long-term benefits of doing it.

ENTJs are strategic, long-term planners who will do almost anything to guarantee themselves a better future. If you sell an ENTJ on the long-term benefits of getting a specific task done, they'll be implementing plans for it before you can finish saying, "Please."

INTJ – Tell them that nobody can figure out the best way to get it done.

INTJs are the ultimate optimizers. They are able to pinpoint the most efficient way to do just about anything, and they often grow frustrated by others' blatant inability to do the same. If you want a task done in the best way possible, give it to an INTJ. And let them know that you're relying on their competence.

ESFJ – Tell them that someone they love needs it done.

There's almost nothing an ESFJ wouldn't do to help out a loved one in need. This type takes immediate action to support the people they're close to and if the task at hand is going to improve someone's circumstances, they'll be on it. No questions asked (Okay, a few questions asked).

ISFJ – Tell them you're counting on them to get it done.

ISFJs take the commitments they make to others incredibly seriously. If you tell them that a given task falls on their shoulders and that you're relying on them to complete it, they'll strive endlessly to make sure it gets done. This type is loyal above all else.

ESFP – Tell them how impressed others will be if they do it.

ESFPs love the spotlight –and consequently, they are willing to go out on a limb to achieve it. If you explain how completing a given task will earn them the limelight and make them seem impressive to others, the ESFP will be clamoring to complete it in no time.

ISFP – Tell them that only the most creative people are capable of getting it done.

ISFPs have an entirely unique world-view and they know it. By telling this type that you need a creative spin to be taken on a particular project, you'll ensure that they'll step up to the plate. They harness any chance to shine creatively.

ISTJ – Tell them nobody else is going to do it unless they do.

ISTJs are the ultimate duty-fulfillers and they understand that most of the important things in life just won't get done unless they do it themselves. Does this make them bitter? Sometimes. But does it also make them efficient workers? Absolutely. Tell an ISTJ that a task rests squarely on their shoulders and you can bet your ass they'll hustle to get it completed.

ESTJ – Tell them the immediate, tangible benefits of doing it.

ESTJs are all about doing what works. If you are able to provide them with a list of clear, tangible outcomes of getting a task done, nothing will stand in their way of completing it. This type is ceaselessly action-oriented and if they see a logical reason to complete a given project, they'll already be working on doing so.

ISTP – Tell them there's a shortcut to getting it done.

ISTPs are the masters of analyzing and finding loopholes within systems. If you tell them there's a quick, painless method of getting something done, they'll be all over finding that method. And then using it to complete the task at hand.

ESTP – Tell them they're the only ones capable of doing it.

ESTPs like to think of themselves as superheroes. Straight-shooters by nature, this type has no problem taking immediate action to get just about any task done – so long as they see a reason to do it. And telling them they're the only ones who can is almost always reason enough.

INFJ – Tell them you need their insight to help get it done.

INFJs understand the world around them in a unique, insightful manner. And they want to use that insight to help the people they love. When you ask this type to help you by providing insight into what you're attempting, you're both playing to their strengths and engaging their empathetic nature. Their inner motivation will rile.

ENFJ – Tell them you need guidance to help get it done.

ENFJs aim to serve as all-knowing mentors to those around them. The #1 way to motivate them is to act as though their guidance is essential to accomplishing a given task or project. They'll jump at the chance to teach you what they know and help you reach your target.

INFP – Tell them it needs to be done in a unique and unprecedented way.

INFPs are wildly creative and take pride in their ability to see things from unique, artistic angles that others simply cannot seem to grasp. If you tell them that a task requires a special artistic flare in order to complete it, they will eagerly step up to bat. Creative endeavours are this type's time to shine.

ENFP – Tell them that if anyone can do it, it's them.

ENFPs thrive on feelings of empowerment. They want to impress and inspire others at all costs, so if you suggest that there's a challenge only they can rise to, it's the surest way of getting them on board. They're eager to prove themselves and show the world that their wildest dreams can become a reality.

CHAPTER 35.

EACH PERSONALITY TYPE'S KRYPTONITE

ENTP – Indecision

ENTPs are enthused about life in almost every capacity – they love planning for the future, speculating over the present and evaluating the past. The world is an all-you-can-eat-buffet for this highly ambitious type and yet they can never decide on just one dish. As excitable as they are ambitious, the ENTP often finds themselves torn between various projects, goals and undertakings, unable to commit to just one. Indecision is the one thing that holds this type back from truly excelling – you might say it is their kryptonite.

INTP – Inaction

INTPs see the world in an objective, rational and creative fashion – a mixture of perceptions that almost no other type shares. However, the INTP is often so busy contemplating and readjusting their worldview that they forget to apply their perceptions to real-world actions. The disinclination to act on their thoughts and ideas is the INTP's kryptonite.

ENTJ – Competitiveness

ENTJs see a direct route to everything they want – and what they want is to be the best at everything. While this highly resourceful type is prone to dominating opponents at much of what they do, the urge to win can occasionally get the better of them. They may find themselves ignoring the long-term consequences of many of their actions as they fight to keep the upper hand in the short-term. The desire to always be on top (rather than to play the long game) is the ENTJ's kryptonite.

INTJ – Sociality

INTJs are brilliant individuals who can reason their way through just about any situation – except social situations. Before their introverted feeling is developed, INTJs often experience difficulty picking up on social nuances, which makes navigating the external world a challenge for them. They may see a clear path to the implementation of their goals, but if they must network or win over people to get there, they will experience difficulty along the way. Socialization is the one realm that logic does not always apply to, and it is therefore INTJ's personal kryptonite.

ESFJ – Obedience

ESFJs are incredibly in tune with the norms, values and expectations of the social world that surrounds them. They are tirelessly careful to not violate any social rules and as a result are often obedient to others' expectations, even when they are not in complete agreement with them. Learning to stand up for themselves – even if it means violating a social or societal rule – is something the ESFJ needs to work on throughout their lives if they do not want their personal kryptonite to rob them of the things they want most.

ISFJ – Self-sacrifice

ISFJs are down-to-earth, focused and capable – but they're also self-sacrificing to a fault. This type has a tendency to internalize almost everything that happens to and around them – therefore taking on responsibility for problems that don't necessarily involve them. The tendency to adopt external problems as their own is the ISFJ's kryptonite.

ESFP – The need for approval

ESFPs have fiercely engaging personalities – this is both their greatest strength and their greatest setback. Though this type is capable of achieving just about anything they set their mind to, they also feel the compulsive need to have everyone around them like them – which occasionally makes them back down from situations that they ought to stand their ground in. The need for approval is in part what makes the ESFP so successful, but it is in equal part their personal kryptonite.

ISFP – Sensitivity

The ISFP's sensitivity is what makes them brilliantly creative and unique – but it's also what holds them back in many ways. Because this type dislikes conflict so intensely, they have a tendency to run for the hills as soon as they foresee a tense situation arising – holding them back from pursuing many relationships or opportunities that could otherwise be beneficial for them. This type's sensitive nature is one of their greatest strengths but their aversion to criticism or conflict is their Achilles heel.

ISTJ – Change

ISTJs are all about quality. They want to use the tried and true method of getting everything done – because why take a chance on something that hasn't proven itself to be reliable? Though this quality is useful for the ISTJ in many ways, it also makes them highly resistant to change. They have trouble believing without seeing, so they often resist changes until they've had enough time to concretely witness the positive outcomes of the change – by which point, the rest of society has already moved onto something new.

ESTJ – Subjectivity

ESTJs are incredibly logical individuals who truly believe that they see the world in the most clear, objective fashion possible. What this type often fails to realize, however, is that their value judgments of the world are highly subjective. What they deem as important is not what the next person deems as important and vice versa. Failing to realize this, the ESTJ often spends a great deal of time frustrated with others for behaving illogically. If this highly rational type were a little more comfortable with accepting that everyone looks at the world differently, they'd be able to save time on lecturing others and use that time to get more shit done.

ISTP – Passiveness

ISTPs are incredibly analytical thinkers, who

can quickly determine the most direct route to getting something done. However, this type prefers analyzing systems to acting on them – which means that many of their brilliant ideas never come to fruition. Despite being incredibly capable individuals by nature, the ISTP's passiveness often causes them to underperform.

ESTP – Impulsivity

ESTPs are incredibly resourceful and capable – but their impulsivity often gets the better of them, causing them to cave into short-term desires rather than pursuing long-term achievements. A quick, on-the-fly reaction time is at the core of this type's personality – but it's also their Achilles heel.

INFJ – Perfectionism

INFJs aren't perfectionists in the stereotypical sense of the word – they aren't the most detail-oriented type nor are they the most outright neurotic. However, they are prone to deliberating over their options to a detrimental extent – trying so hard to pinpoint the best of all possible options that they end up missing out on opportunities altogether. Attempting to always seek out the most perfect situation – and refusing to take a chance on anything less – is the INFJ's Achilles heel.

ENFJ – The Urge To Interfere

ENFJs are highly perceptive individuals, who usually have a keen grasp on what is likely to help or hinder their loved ones. As a consequence, they often feel compelled to intervene in the lives of their loved ones, perceiving themselves to know what's best for them. This can not only lead to tension and conflict if the ENFJ is not careful, but it will also exhaust them to the core as they try to care for everyone around them at all times. The compulsion to help those who are struggling is the ENFJ's personal kryptonite.

INFP – Idealization Of Others

People, situations, opportunities, problems – you name it, the INFP can idealize it. This type lives largely inside their own minds and while their wild imaginations help them in many ways, they can also create a disconnect between the INFP and reality, particularly in the arena of love. It is their proneness to idealizing potential partners that so often breaks apart INFP relationships before they even begin – when the other person fails to live up to the standard the INFP had created for them internally. The urge to distort reality with fantasy is the INFP's kryptonite.

ENFP – The 'Greener Grass' Syndrome

ENFPs are ceaselessly scanning the horizons for new, exciting opportunities that they haven't tried yet. Even when they're perfectly content with their lives, this enthusiastic type is prone to abandoning a good thing in favor of the next, potentially better thing. Their never-ending quest for the next great thrill – and their corresponding aversion to stick with what they love – is the ENFP's Achilles heel.

CHAPTER 36.

EACH PERSONALITY TYPE'S SUPERPOWER

ENTP – Outside-The-Box Thinking

Of all the personality types, ENTPs are perhaps the most genuinely open-minded. This insatiably curious type enjoys examining issues from every available angle – which consequently allows them to come up with the most unique and impressive solutions that are available for any given problem. If ENTPs were superheroes, their superpower would be unconventional thinking and problem-solving abilities.

INTP – Objectivity

INTPs are the ultimate skeptics of the world.

This type refuses to settle for cookie-cutter explanations of absolutely anything and they are incredibly thorough in all their intellectual pursuits. If INTPs were superheroes, their greatest strength would lie in their ability to analyze situations objectively and rationally – taking personal biases out of the equation in order to determine what's really going on.

ENTJ – Decisiveness

If the ENTJ were a superhero, they'd be *'Get Shit Done (Wo)Man."* This highly capable type keeps a cool head and a rational mind while under pressure – they are always capable of making difficult decisions with swift, rational ease. This type's superpower lies in their unique ability to make clearheaded, outcome-optimized choices while everyone around them is losing their heads.

INTJ – Clarity

The INTJ's greatest strength lies in their ability to remove the 'outside noise' from their perceptions of the world and get right down to the heart of any given situation. This type sees things clearly, intuitively and precisely – naturally understanding how the world works in a holistic framework. If INTJ's were superheroes, their greatest strength would lie in their ability to intuitively understand how the world around them functions, while everyone else remains caught up in the trivialities of day-to-day living.

ESFJ – Preparedness

ESFJs are ruthlessly organized. This type is prepared for almost any worst-case scenario that could possibly arise, which means that in an emergency, you'd want them by your side. If ESFJs were superheroes, their superpower would be caring for those around them through their superior sense of preparedness… which is already what they do in their everyday lives. ESFJs truly are our natural everyday heroes.

ISFJ – Loyalty

In a world of crooked villains and volatile heroes, ISFJs prevail as the most loyal and devoted of all personalities. This unlikely hero will fight for any cause they have committed to until the bitter end. Their strong sense of duty and devotion is what sets ISFJs apart from the other types – their superhero alter-ego would undoubtedly be the last (wo)man standing in the face of any external treachery.

ESFP – Charm

If any type is inherently blessed with the 'gift of the gab,' it's the ESFP. This type has an effortless knack for understanding others and catering to exactly what they want to hear. Brilliant charmers and salespeople, the ESFP's superpower truly lies in their ability to win over others. Socialization is their natural second nature.

ISFP – Individualism

ISFPs are blatantly unafraid to show their true colors to the world – this type is inventive, unconventional and individualistic to a fault. In a world full of mindless drones, the ISFP refuses to ever conform. Their superpower is individualism – the ability to stay true to themselves despite external pressure to change.

ISTJ – Accuracy

ISTJs are incredibly adept at pinpointing the best or most correct way of going about almost anything. This type relies on only the most practical ways of getting things done, which is a skill that much of society lacks. If ISTJs were superheroes, their superpower would be the ability to pinpoint the most accurate method of getting things done, while everyone else is wasting their time on futile trial-and-error methods.

ESTJ – Efficiency

ESTJs are incredibly decisive folk. They waste no time when it comes to implementing and executing good ideas, in the most efficient way possible. If this type were a superhero, their superpower would be efficiency – the ability to actually get things done while everyone else is freaking out about the details.

ISTP – Hacking

ISTPs invented the phenomenon of 'life hacks.' This type sees the quickest and most hassle-free way of getting just about everything done. They are able to figure out new systems with ease, and quickly pinpoint any shortcuts that might be available within them. If the ISTP were a superhero, they'd be 'Shortcut (Wo)man' – saving the world one life hack at a time.

ESTP – Capability

In a world full of deliberators and worriers, ESTPs are the least afraid to take action on what they want. Undaunted by the rules or formal procedures, this straight-shooting type is often quick to go after their goals. If they were superheroes, they'd be 'Capable (Wo)man' – the hero who just goes out and does the thing, while everyone else stays home and freaks out about nothing.

INFJ – Foresight

INFJs possess the impressive ability to predict

how a given situation is going to turn out for almost everyone involved. While some equate this ability to ESP, INFJs know that it is due to their natural people-intuition combining with their future-focused thinking. Understanding others on a deep level, the INFJ is often able to predict how they'll act in the future and what the corresponding results of their decisions will be. If the INFJs were superheroes, their superpower would be the ability to predict others' actions.

ENFJ – Leadership

Perhaps more than any other type, ENFJs possess the unique ability to rally and win over others. Their natural confidence and people-intuition allows the ENFJ to emerge as a natural leader in most situations. If they were superheroes, the ENFJ's superpower would be persuasion and guidance – they have a natural inclination to lead others to greatness.

INFP – Wisdom

INFPs are the ultimate 'old souls.' From a very

young age, this type is keenly aware of the emotional truths that surround them and they can tune into these perceptions almost effortlessly. If INFPs were superheroes, they would be the wise sages who possess the unique ability to see the root of all human conflict and struggle.

ENFP – Inspiration

ENFPs are the ultimate optimists – they see the best in everything they do and everyone they meet – and they possess the unique ability to inspire the best in others. This type's endless enthusiasm for the world around them – combined with their ability to chase and achieve their dreams – is incredibly motivating to those around them. If ENFPs were superheroes, their superpower would be inspiration.

CHAPTER 37.

WHAT WE FORGET TO THANK EACH MYERS-BRIGGS PERSONALITY TYPE FOR

ENTP: Thank you for reminding us that there are a thousand ways of getting around any problem and that we are never, ever stuck.

INTP: Thank you for remaining as open-minded and tolerant as you are intelligent.

ENTJ: Thank you for always pushing us to reach our full potential.

INTJ: Thank you for sharing your unique worldview with us, with patience and depth.

ESFJ: Thank you for taking care of us during the times when we cannot take care of ourselves.

ISFJ: Thank you for offering your huge, selfless heart to others without ever asking for anything in return.

ESFP: Thank you for making life an adventure.

ISFP: Thank you for reminding us what a beautiful world we live in whenever we're at risk of forgetting it.

ISTJ: Thank you for being somebody we can always rely on.

ESTJ: Thank you for protecting and sheltering the people you love.

ISTP: Thank you for intricately understanding how basically everything works, so that the rest of us do not have to.

ESTP: Thank you for reminding us that so many risks are worth taking.

INFJ: Thank you for helping us see what we need out of life and the future when we cannot see it ourselves.

ENFJ: Thank you for helping us to realize our own greatest strengths.

INFP: Thank you for knowing all the darkest parts of us and loving us anyway.

ENFP: Thank you for believing in us even when we do not believe in ourselves.

ABOUT THE AUTHOR

Heidi Priebe graduated from the University of Guelph, Ontario with a degree in Psychology and the firm ambition to prove her skeptical professors wrong about the Myers-Briggs Type Indicator. When she's not blogging about the sixteen types, Heidi enjoys reading, traveling and deleting heated emails from disgruntled anti-Jung psychologists. She is a textbook ENFP, which she explains in her other book, *The Comprehensive ENFP Survival Guide.*

Made in the USA
Middletown, DE
17 May 2016